HOUSEPETS
CAN BE REAL
LADYKILLERS.

In which lies an account of animals
who walk about on two legs.

Sona si Latine loqueris

To which is added
An ACCOUNT of an

ADORABLE
C O R G I

I mean look at him.

—— *Nupperime de Gallia huc volavi!*
Mehercule, bracchia mea defatiga sunt!
Rodnicus Dangerfieldicus.

CHARLESTON
Printed for *Rick Griffin*, at *Createſpace*,
MMXII.

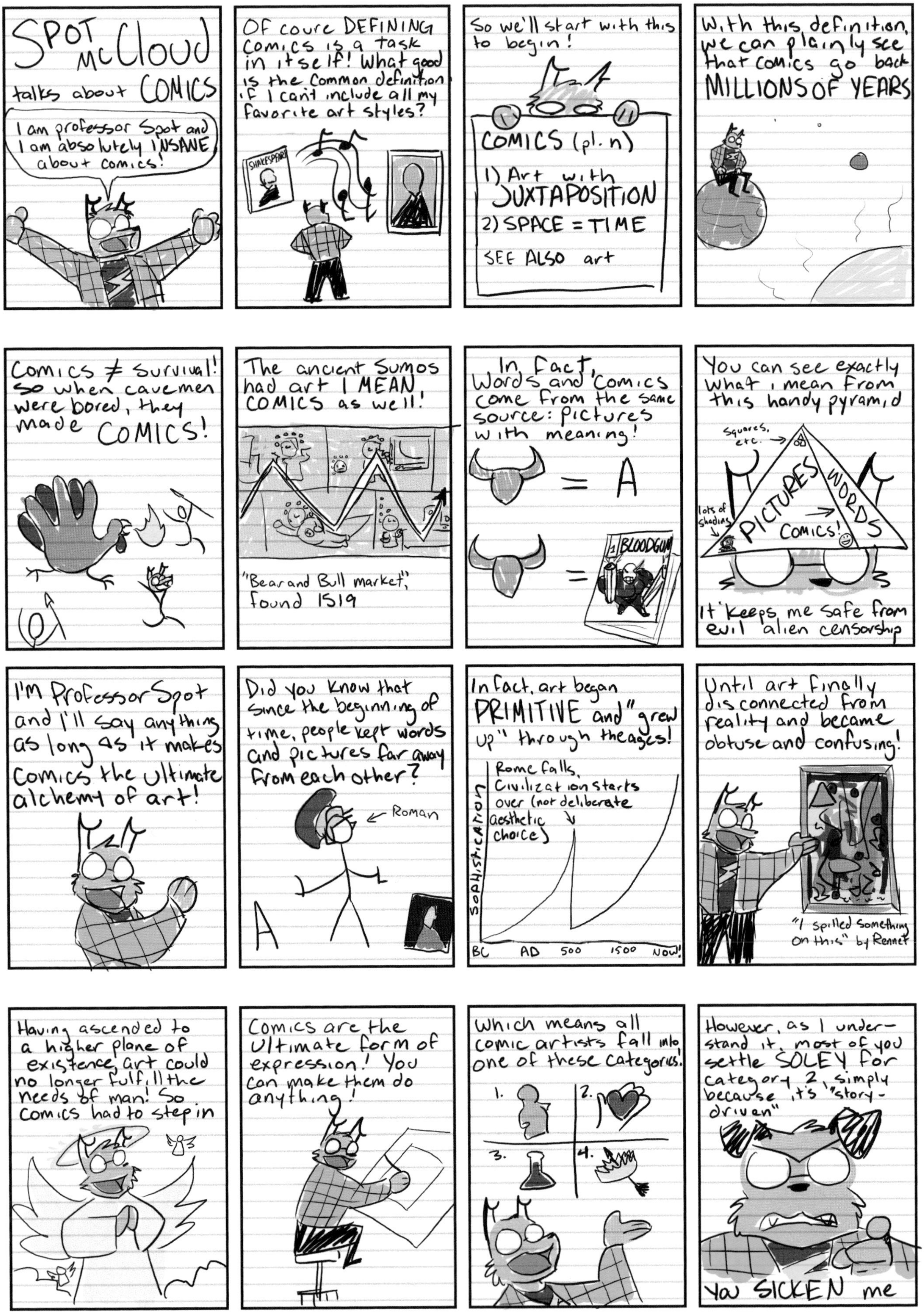

SPOT McCloud talks about COMICS
I am professor Spot and I am absolutely INSANE about comics!
Of coure DEFINING comics is a task in itself! What good is the common definition if I can't include all my favorite art styles?
SHAKESPEARE
So we'll start with this to begin!
COMICS (pl. n)
1) Art with JUXTAPOSITION
2) SPACE = TIME
SEE ALSO art
With this definition, we can plainly see that comics go back MILLIONS OF YEARS
Comics ≠ survival! so when cavemen were bored, they made COMICS!
The ancient Sumos had art I MEAN COMICS as well!
"Bear and Bull market", found 1519
In fact, Words and Comics come from the same source: pictures with meaning!
= A
BLOODGUM
You can see exactly what I mean from this handy pyramid
Squares, etc.
lots of shading
PICTURES
WORDS
COMICS!
It keeps me safe from evil alien censorship
I'm Professor Spot and I'll say anything as long as it makes Comics the ultimate alchemy of art!
Did you know that since the beginning of time, people kept words and pictures far away from each other?
Roman
A
In fact, art began PRIMITIVE and "grew up" through the ages!
Rome falls, Civilization starts over (not deliberate aesthetic choice)
SOPHISTICATION
BC
AD
500
1500
NOW!
Until art finally disconnected from reality and became obtuse and confusing!
"I spilled something on this" by Rennet
Having ascended to a higher plane of existence, art could no longer fulfill the needs of man! So comics had to step in
Comics are the ultimate form of expression! You can make them do anything!
Which means all comic artists fall into one of these categories!
1.
2.
3.
4.
However, as I understand it, most of you settle SOLEY for category 2, simply because it's "story-driven"
You SICKEN me

In the future, comics on the nets will expand our horizons!

monetization is EASY with micropayments! by the year 2005, it will become standard business practice

insert 1¢ for next panel

But even more than that, we can escape the restrictions of print with...

EXPLOSION

INFINITE

CANVAS

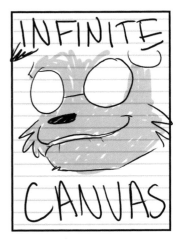

Not only does it take advantage of the UNLIMITED page space, but it's also impossible to anthologize!

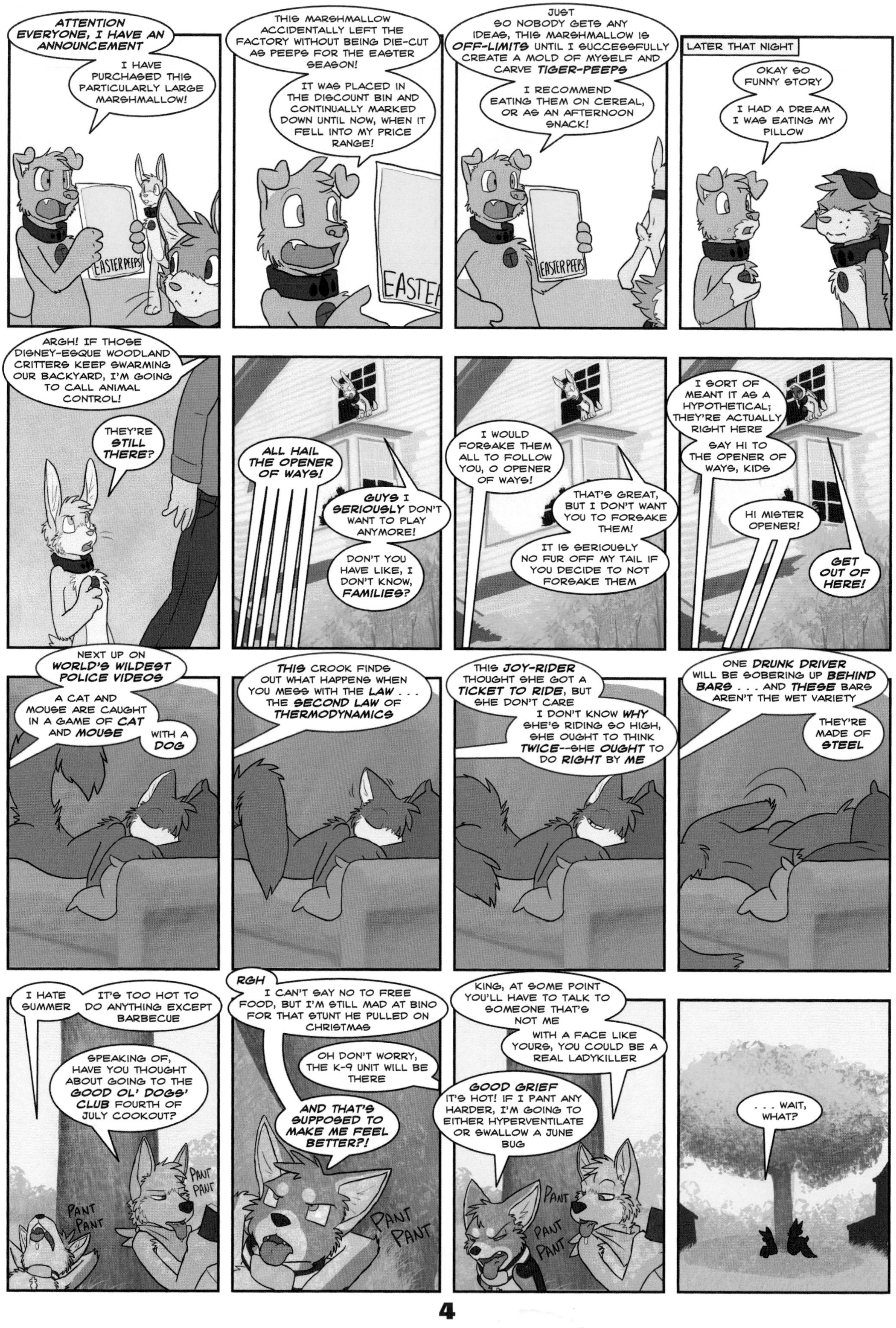
ATTENTION EVERYONE, I HAVE AN ANNOUNCEMENT
I HAVE PURCHASED THIS PARTICULARLY LARGE MARSHMALLOW!
EASTER PEEPS
THIS MARSHMALLOW ACCIDENTALLY LEFT THE FACTORY WITHOUT BEING DIE-CUT AS PEEPS FOR THE EASTER SEASON!
IT WAS PLACED IN THE DISCOUNT BIN AND CONTINUALLY MARKED DOWN UNTIL NOW, WHEN IT FELL INTO MY PRICE RANGE!
EASTER
JUST SO NOBODY GETS ANY IDEAS, THIS MARSHMALLOW IS OFF-LIMITS UNTIL I SUCCESSFULLY CREATE A MOLD OF MYSELF AND CARVE TIGER-PEEPS
I RECOMMEND EATING THEM ON CEREAL, OR AS AN AFTERNOON SNACK!
EASTER PEEPS
LATER THAT NIGHT
OKAY SO FUNNY STORY
I HAD A DREAM I WAS EATING MY PILLOW
ARGH! IF THOSE DISNEY-ESQUE WOODLAND CRITTERS KEEP SWARMING OUR BACKYARD, I'M GOING TO CALL ANIMAL CONTROL!
THEY'RE STILL THERE?
ALL HAIL THE OPENER OF WAYS!
GUYS I SERIOUSLY DON'T WANT TO PLAY ANYMORE!
DON'T YOU HAVE LIKE, I DON'T KNOW, FAMILIES?
I WOULD FORSAKE THEM ALL TO FOLLOW YOU, O OPENER OF WAYS!
THAT'S GREAT, BUT I DON'T WANT YOU TO FORSAKE THEM!
IT IS SERIOUSLY NO FUR OFF MY TAIL IF YOU DECIDE TO NOT FORSAKE THEM
I SORT OF MEANT IT AS A HYPOTHETICAL; THEY'RE ACTUALLY RIGHT HERE
SAY HI TO THE OPENER OF WAYS, KIDS
HI MISTER OPENER!
GET OUT OF HERE!
NEXT UP ON WORLD'S WILDEST POLICE VIDEOS
A CAT AND MOUSE ARE CAUGHT IN A GAME OF CAT AND MOUSE
WITH A DOG
THIS CROOK FINDS OUT WHAT HAPPENS WHEN YOU MESS WITH THE LAW . . . THE SECOND LAW OF THERMODYNAMICS
THIS JOY-RIDER THOUGHT SHE GOT A TICKET TO RIDE, BUT SHE DON'T CARE
I DON'T KNOW WHY SHE'S RIDING SO HIGH, SHE OUGHT TO THINK TWICE--SHE OUGHT TO DO RIGHT BY ME
ONE DRUNK DRIVER WILL BE SOBERING UP BEHIND BARS . . . AND THESE BARS AREN'T THE WET VARIETY
THEY'RE MADE OF STEEL
I HATE SUMMER
IT'S TOO HOT TO DO ANYTHING EXCEPT BARBECUE
SPEAKING OF, HAVE YOU THOUGHT ABOUT GOING TO THE GOOD OL' DOGS' CLUB FOURTH OF JULY COOKOUT?
PANT PANT
PANT PANT
RGH
I CAN'T SAY NO TO FREE FOOD, BUT I'M STILL MAD AT BINO FOR THAT STUNT HE PULLED ON CHRISTMAS
OH DON'T WORRY, THE K-9 UNIT WILL BE THERE
AND THAT'S SUPPOSED TO MAKE ME FEEL BETTER?!
PANT PANT
KING, AT SOME POINT YOU'LL HAVE TO TALK TO SOMEONE THAT'S NOT ME
WITH A FACE LIKE YOURS, YOU COULD BE A REAL LADYKILLER
GOOD GRIEF
IT'S HOT! IF I PANT ANY HARDER, I'M GOING TO EITHER HYPERVENTILATE OR SWALLOW A JUNE BUG
PANT
PANT PANT
. . . WAIT, WHAT?

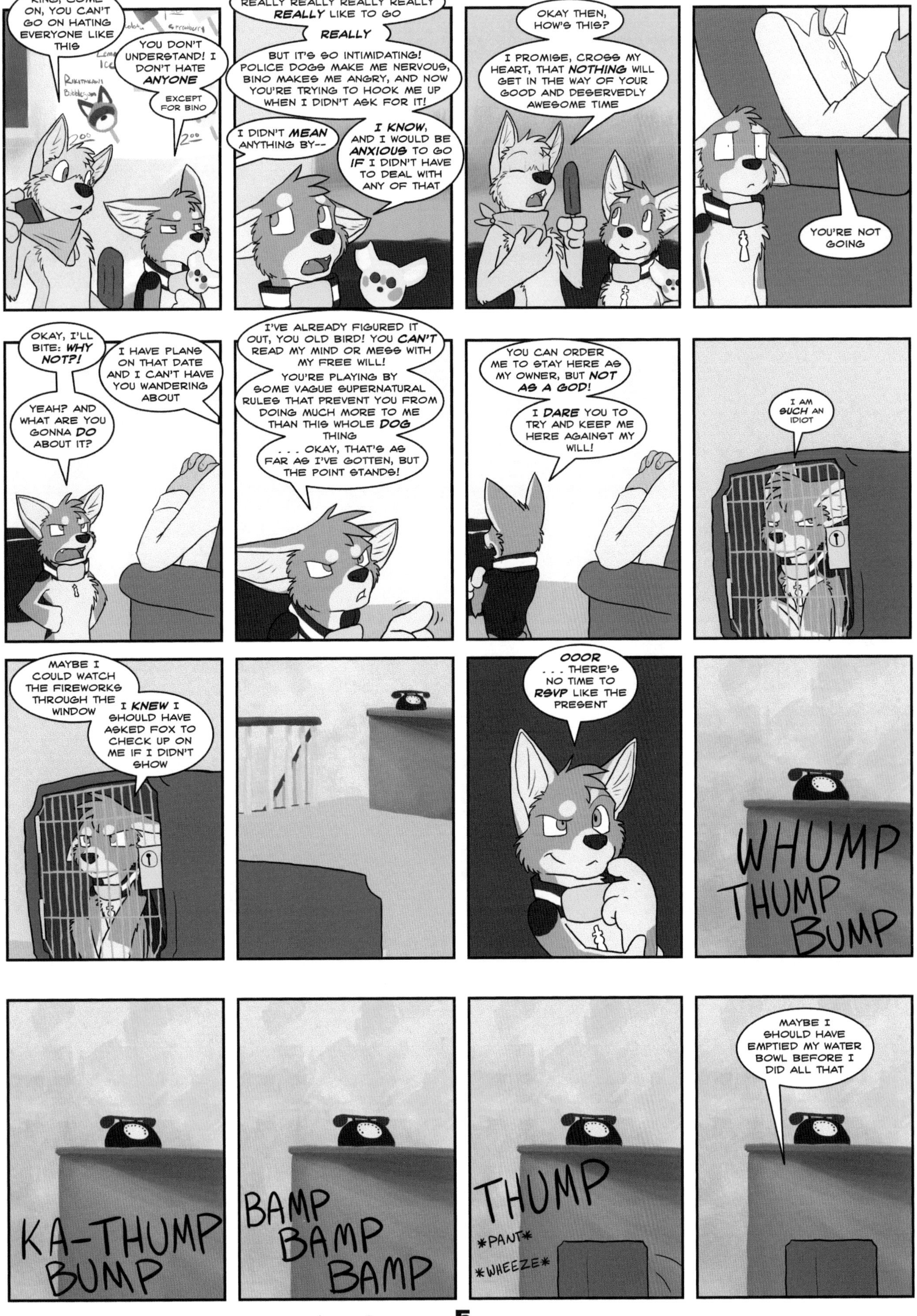
KING, COME ON, YOU CAN'T GO ON HATING EVERYONE LIKE THIS
YOU DON'T UNDERSTAND! I DON'T HATE ANYONE
EXCEPT FOR BINO
SERIOUSLY, I WOULD REALLY REALLY REALLY REALLY REALLY LIKE TO GO
REALLY
BUT IT'S SO INTIMIDATING! POLICE DOGS MAKE ME NERVOUS, BINO MAKES ME ANGRY, AND NOW YOU'RE TRYING TO HOOK ME UP WHEN I DIDN'T ASK FOR IT!
I DIDN'T MEAN ANYTHING BY--
I KNOW, AND I WOULD BE ANXIOUS TO GO IF I DIDN'T HAVE TO DEAL WITH ANY OF THAT
OKAY THEN, HOW'S THIS?
I PROMISE, CROSS MY HEART, THAT NOTHING WILL GET IN THE WAY OF YOUR GOOD AND DESERVEDLY AWESOME TIME
YOU'RE NOT GOING
OKAY, I'LL BITE: WHY NOT?!
I HAVE PLANS ON THAT DATE AND I CAN'T HAVE YOU WANDERING ABOUT
YEAH? AND WHAT ARE YOU GONNA DO ABOUT IT?
I'VE ALREADY FIGURED IT OUT, YOU OLD BIRD! YOU CAN'T READ MY MIND OR MESS WITH MY FREE WILL!
YOU'RE PLAYING BY SOME VAGUE SUPERNATURAL RULES THAT PREVENT YOU FROM DOING MUCH MORE TO ME THAN THIS WHOLE DOG THING
. . . OKAY, THAT'S AS FAR AS I'VE GOTTEN, BUT THE POINT STANDS!
YOU CAN ORDER ME TO STAY HERE AS MY OWNER, BUT NOT AS A GOD!
I DARE YOU TO TRY AND KEEP ME HERE AGAINST MY WILL!
I AM SUCH AN IDIOT
MAYBE I COULD WATCH THE FIREWORKS THROUGH THE WINDOW
I KNEW I SHOULD HAVE ASKED FOX TO CHECK UP ON ME IF I DIDN'T SHOW
OOOR
. . . THERE'S NO TIME TO RSVP LIKE THE PRESENT
WHUMP THUMP BUMP
KA-THUMP BUMP
BAMP BAMP BAMP
THUMP
PANT
WHEEZE
MAYBE I SHOULD HAVE EMPTIED MY WATER BOWL BEFORE I DID ALL THAT

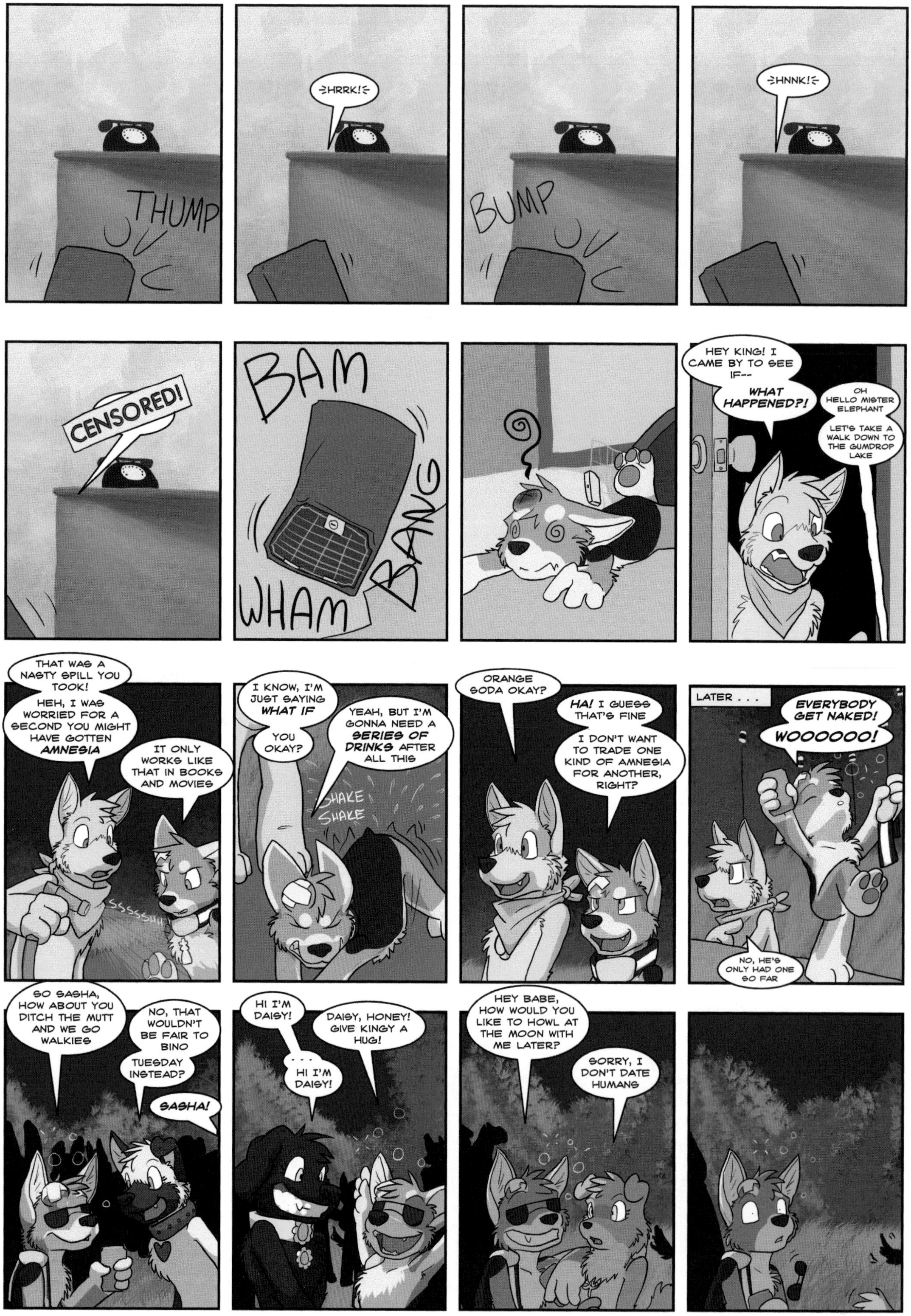
THUMP
HRRK!
BUMP
HNNK!
CENSORED!
BAM
WHAM
BANG
HEY KING! I CAME BY TO SEE IF--
WHAT HAPPENED?!
OH HELLO MISTER ELEPHANT
LET'S TAKE A WALK DOWN TO THE GUMDROP LAKE
THAT WAS A NASTY SPILL YOU TOOK!
HEH, I WAS WORRIED FOR A SECOND YOU MIGHT HAVE GOTTEN AMNESIA
IT ONLY WORKS LIKE THAT IN BOOKS AND MOVIES
SSSSSHH
I KNOW, I'M JUST SAYING WHAT IF
YOU OKAY?
YEAH, BUT I'M GONNA NEED A SERIES OF DRINKS AFTER ALL THIS
SHAKE SHAKE
ORANGE SODA OKAY?
HA! I GUESS THAT'S FINE
I DON'T WANT TO TRADE ONE KIND OF AMNESIA FOR ANOTHER, RIGHT?
LATER . . .
EVERYBODY GET NAKED!
WOOOOOO!
NO, HE'S ONLY HAD ONE SO FAR
SO SASHA, HOW ABOUT YOU DITCH THE MUTT AND WE GO WALKIES
NO, THAT WOULDN'T BE FAIR TO BINO
TUESDAY INSTEAD?
SASHA!
HI I'M DAISY!
DAISY, HONEY! GIVE KINGY A HUG!
. . .
HI I'M DAISY!
HEY BABE, HOW WOULD YOU LIKE TO HOWL AT THE MOON WITH ME LATER?
SORRY, I DON'T DATE HUMANS

OKAY KING GET A HOLD OF YOURSELF

GET A HOLD OF YOURSELF

ONE OF THEM KNOWS YOUR SECRET

WHY?!

AND STOP FLIRTING

SAY, UH, *CAT*, YOU WOULDN'T HAPPEN TO KNOW WHO THAT BEAUTIFUL DOG IS, SHE'S SHORT, HAS A GREEN COLLAR WITH THE EYE OF RA?

OH, THAT'S TAROT! I DIDN'T KNOW SHE WAS HERE

I WAS HITTING ON HER AND SHE SAID SOME REALLY WEIRD STUFF, DO YOU KNOW WHY?

THAT'S BECAUSE SHE'S PSYCHIC, LIKE A DOLPHIN? ONLY SHE CAN *READ* MINDS TOO

OH, OKAY, THAT'S A PERFECTLY NORMAL EXPLANATION

ALSO SHE IS MY BEST FRIEND'S GIRLFRIEND

YOU HAVE FIVE SECONDS UNTIL YOUR APPENDAGES START COMING OFF

OH HEY LOOK THAT SODA WENT RIGHT TO MY BLADDER HAHA SEE YA

HAVE YOU SEEN TAROT? CUTE LITTLE POMERANIAN I THINK IS WHAT THE BREED IS CALLED?

OH, I SAW SOMEONE LIKE THAT WALK INTO THE WOODS JUST OVER THERE

TAROT! HEY TAROT!

HEY! YOU'RE GONNA MISS THE FIREWORKS!

I'M SORRY FOR HITTING ON YOU!

COME BACK! PLEASE!

I NEED SOMEONE WHO UNDERSTANDS . . .

DIDN'T I TELL YOU TO STAY AT HOME?

HEHE, OH SODA, WHAT WALK IN THE WOODS AT NIGHT *WON'T* YOU MAKE ABSOLUTELY HORRIFYING?

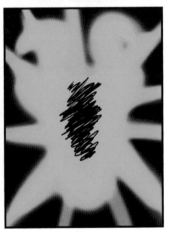

YOU'RE GOING TO RUIN EVERYTHING!

YIPE

DONK

PETE! STOP THIS AT ONCE

YOU? BUT YOU'RE . . .

SO IT WAS YOU WHO CALLED ME HERE

YOU'VE BEEN ABUSING THE RULES, PETE

NAUGHTY, NAUGHTY BIRDIE

THIS WOULD BE SO AWESOME IF I DIDN'T JUST WET MYSELF

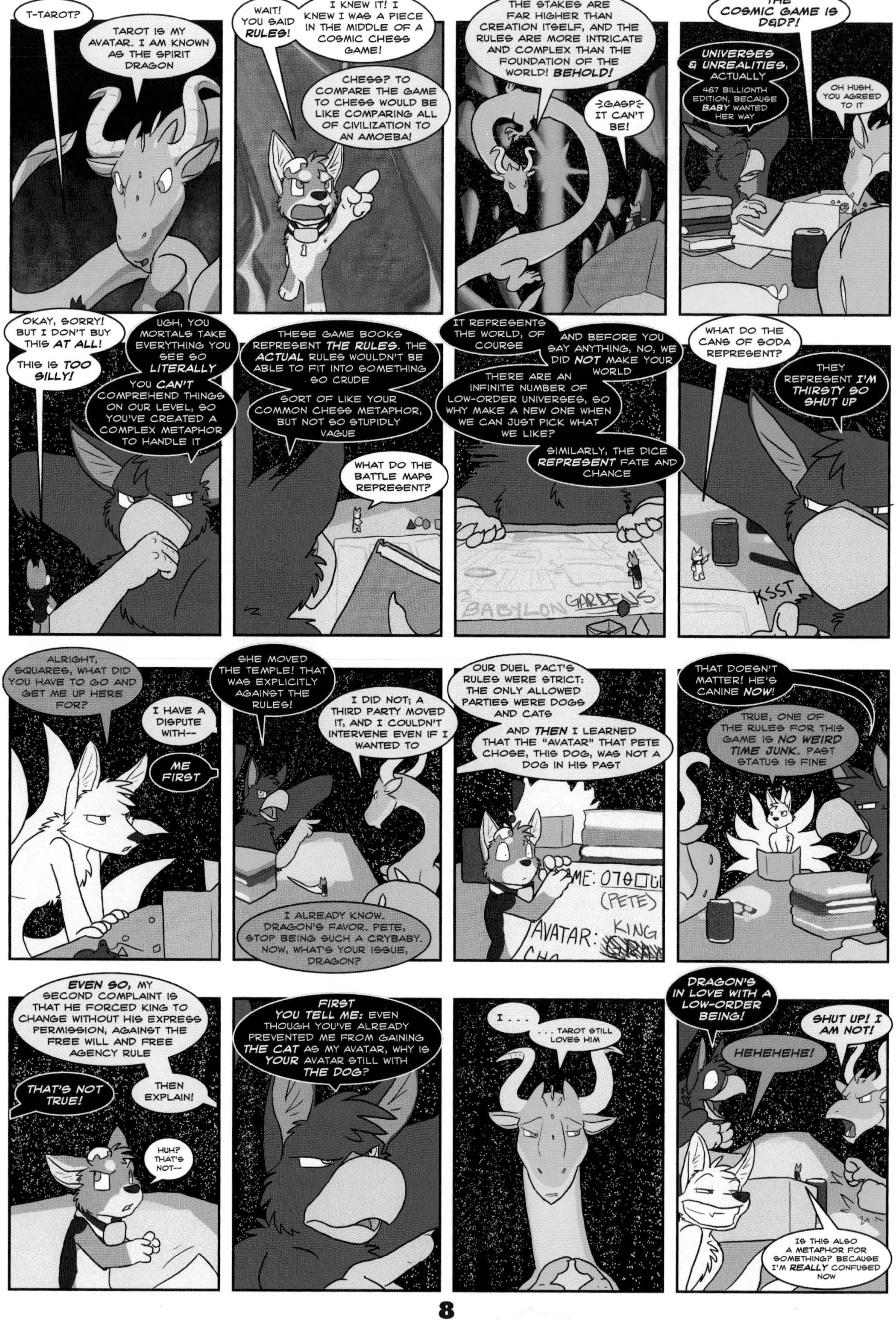
T-TAROT?
TAROT IS MY AVATAR. I AM KNOWN AS THE SPIRIT DRAGON
WAIT! YOU SAID RULES!
I KNEW IT! I KNEW I WAS A PIECE IN THE MIDDLE OF A COSMIC CHESS GAME!
CHESS? TO COMPARE THE GAME TO CHESS WOULD BE LIKE COMPARING ALL OF CIVILIZATION TO AN AMOEBA!
THE STAKES ARE FAR HIGHER THAN CREATION ITSELF, AND THE RULES ARE MORE INTRICATE AND COMPLEX THAN THE FOUNDATION OF THE WORLD! BEHOLD!
-GASP- IT CAN'T BE!
THE COSMIC GAME IS D&D?!
UNIVERSES & UNREALITIES, ACTUALLY
467 BILLIONTH EDITION, BECAUSE BABY WANTED HER WAY
OH HUSH. YOU AGREED TO IT
OKAY, SORRY! BUT I DON'T BUY THIS AT ALL!
THIS IS TOO SILLY!
UGH, YOU MORTALS TAKE EVERYTHING YOU SEE SO LITERALLY
YOU CAN'T COMPREHEND THINGS ON OUR LEVEL, SO YOU'VE CREATED A COMPLEX METAPHOR TO HANDLE IT
THESE GAME BOOKS REPRESENT THE RULES. THE ACTUAL RULES WOULDN'T BE ABLE TO FIT INTO SOMETHING SO CRUDE
SORT OF LIKE YOUR COMMON CHESS METAPHOR, BUT NOT SO STUPIDLY VAGUE
WHAT DO THE BATTLE MAPS REPRESENT?
IT REPRESENTS THE WORLD, OF COURSE
AND BEFORE YOU SAY ANYTHING, NO, WE DID NOT MAKE YOUR WORLD
THERE ARE AN INFINITE NUMBER OF LOW-ORDER UNIVERSES, SO WHY MAKE A NEW ONE WHEN WE CAN JUST PICK WHAT WE LIKE?
SIMILARLY, THE DICE REPRESENT FATE AND CHANCE
BABYLON GARDENS
WHAT DO THE CANS OF SODA REPRESENT?
THEY REPRESENT I'M THIRSTY SO SHUT UP
KSST
ALRIGHT, SQUARES, WHAT DID YOU HAVE TO GO AND GET ME UP HERE FOR?
I HAVE A DISPUTE WITH--
ME FIRST
SHE MOVED THE TEMPLE! THAT WAS EXPLICITLY AGAINST THE RULES!
I DID NOT; A THIRD PARTY MOVED IT, AND I COULDN'T INTERVENE EVEN IF I WANTED TO
I ALREADY KNOW. DRAGON'S FAVOR. PETE, STOP BEING SUCH A CRYBABY. NOW, WHAT'S YOUR ISSUE, DRAGON?
OUR DUEL PACT'S RULES WERE STRICT: THE ONLY ALLOWED PARTIES WERE DOGS AND CATS
AND THEN I LEARNED THAT THE "AVATAR" THAT PETE CHOSE, THIS DOG, WAS NOT A DOG IN HIS PAST
(PETE)
AVATAR: KING
THAT DOESN'T MATTER! HE'S CANINE NOW!
TRUE, ONE OF THE RULES FOR THIS GAME IS NO WEIRD TIME JUNK. PAST STATUS IS FINE
EVEN SO, MY SECOND COMPLAINT IS THAT HE FORCED KING TO CHANGE WITHOUT HIS EXPRESS PERMISSION, AGAINST THE FREE WILL AND FREE AGENCY RULE
THAT'S NOT TRUE!
THEN EXPLAIN!
HUH? THAT'S NOT--
FIRST YOU TELL ME: EVEN THOUGH YOU'VE ALREADY PREVENTED ME FROM GAINING THE CAT AS MY AVATAR, WHY IS YOUR AVATAR STILL WITH THE DOG?
I . . .
. . . TAROT STILL LOVES HIM
DRAGON'S IN LOVE WITH A LOW-ORDER BEING!
SHUT UP! I AM NOT!
HEHEHEHE!
IS THIS ALSO A METAPHOR FOR SOMETHING? BECAUSE I'M REALLY CONFUSED NOW

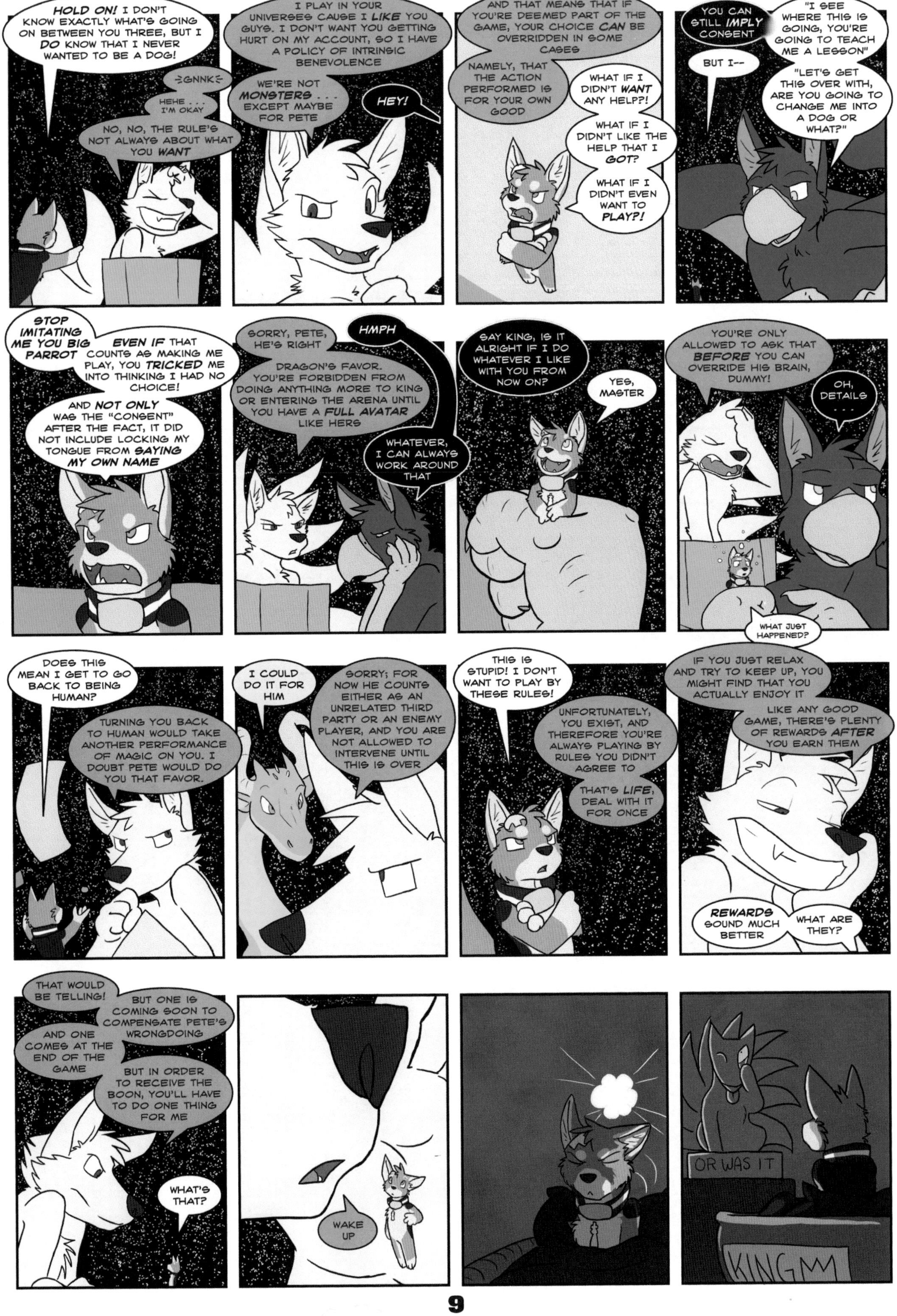

HOLD ON! I DON'T KNOW EXACTLY WHAT'S GOING ON BETWEEN YOU THREE, BUT I DO KNOW THAT I NEVER WANTED TO BE A DOG!
GNNK
HEHE . . . I'M OKAY
NO, NO, THE RULE'S NOT ALWAYS ABOUT WHAT YOU WANT
I PLAY IN YOUR UNIVERSES CAUSE I LIKE YOU GUYS. I DON'T WANT YOU GETTING HURT ON MY ACCOUNT, SO I HAVE A POLICY OF INTRINSIC BENEVOLENCE
WE'RE NOT MONSTERS . . . EXCEPT MAYBE FOR PETE
HEY!
AND THAT MEANS THAT IF YOU'RE DEEMED PART OF THE GAME, YOUR CHOICE CAN BE OVERRIDDEN IN SOME CASES
NAMELY, THAT THE ACTION PERFORMED IS FOR YOUR OWN GOOD
WHAT IF I DIDN'T WANT ANY HELP?!
WHAT IF I DIDN'T LIKE THE HELP THAT I GOT?
WHAT IF I DIDN'T EVEN WANT TO PLAY?!
YOU CAN STILL IMPLY CONSENT
BUT I--
"I SEE WHERE THIS IS GOING, YOU'RE GOING TO TEACH ME A LESSON"
"LET'S GET THIS OVER WITH, ARE YOU GOING TO CHANGE ME INTO A DOG OR WHAT?"
STOP IMITATING ME YOU BIG PARROT
EVEN IF THAT COUNTS AS MAKING ME PLAY, YOU TRICKED ME INTO THINKING I HAD NO CHOICE!
AND NOT ONLY WAS THE "CONSENT" AFTER THE FACT, IT DID NOT INCLUDE LOCKING MY TONGUE FROM SAYING MY OWN NAME
SORRY, PETE, HE'S RIGHT
HMPH
DRAGON'S FAVOR. YOU'RE FORBIDDEN FROM DOING ANYTHING MORE TO KING OR ENTERING THE ARENA UNTIL YOU HAVE A FULL AVATAR LIKE HERS
WHATEVER, I CAN ALWAYS WORK AROUND THAT
SAY KING, IS IT ALRIGHT IF I DO WHATEVER I LIKE WITH YOU FROM NOW ON?
YES, MASTER
YOU'RE ONLY ALLOWED TO ASK THAT BEFORE YOU CAN OVERRIDE HIS BRAIN, DUMMY!
OH, DETAILS . . .
WHAT JUST HAPPENED?
DOES THIS MEAN I GET TO GO BACK TO BEING HUMAN?
TURNING YOU BACK TO HUMAN WOULD TAKE ANOTHER PERFORMANCE OF MAGIC ON YOU. I DOUBT PETE WOULD DO YOU THAT FAVOR.
I COULD DO IT FOR HIM
SORRY; FOR NOW HE COUNTS EITHER AS AN UNRELATED THIRD PARTY OR AN ENEMY PLAYER, AND YOU ARE NOT ALLOWED TO INTERVENE UNTIL THIS IS OVER
THIS IS STUPID! I DON'T WANT TO PLAY BY THESE RULES!
UNFORTUNATELY, YOU EXIST, AND THEREFORE YOU'RE ALWAYS PLAYING BY RULES YOU DIDN'T AGREE TO
THAT'S LIFE, DEAL WITH IT FOR ONCE
IF YOU JUST RELAX AND TRY TO KEEP UP, YOU MIGHT FIND THAT YOU ACTUALLY ENJOY IT
LIKE ANY GOOD GAME, THERE'S PLENTY OF REWARDS AFTER YOU EARN THEM
REWARDS SOUND MUCH BETTER
WHAT ARE THEY?
THAT WOULD BE TELLING!
BUT ONE IS COMING SOON TO COMPENSATE PETE'S WRONGDOING
AND ONE COMES AT THE END OF THE GAME
BUT IN ORDER TO RECEIVE THE BOON, YOU'LL HAVE TO DO ONE THING FOR ME
WHAT'S THAT?
WAKE UP
OR WAS IT
KINGM

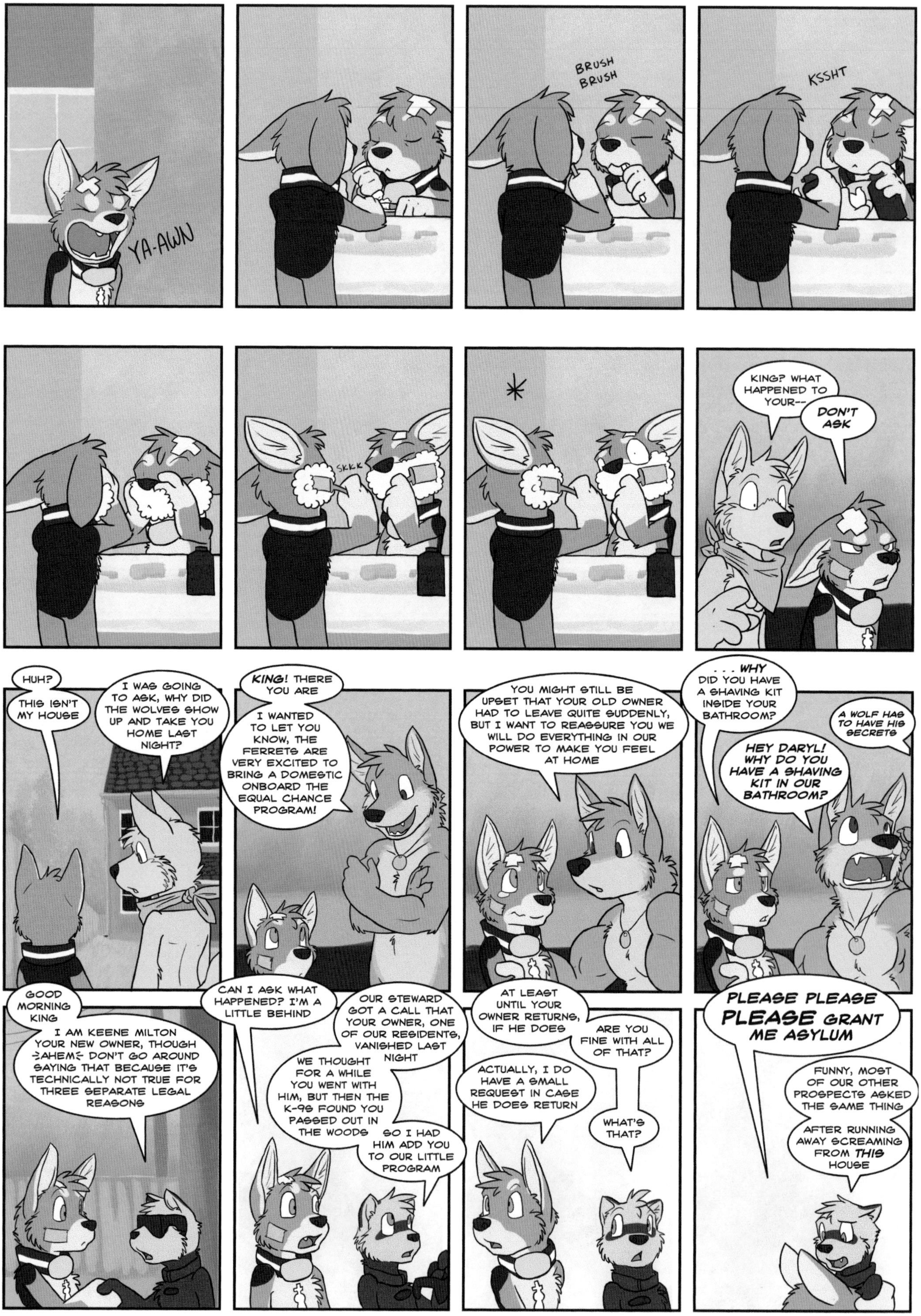

YA-AWN
BRUSH BRUSH
KSSHT
SKKK
KING? WHAT HAPPENED TO YOUR--
DON'T ASK
HUH? THIS ISN'T MY HOUSE
I WAS GOING TO ASK, WHY DID THE WOLVES SHOW UP AND TAKE YOU HOME LAST NIGHT?
KING! THERE YOU ARE
I WANTED TO LET YOU KNOW, THE FERRETS ARE VERY EXCITED TO BRING A DOMESTIC ONBOARD THE EQUAL CHANCE PROGRAM!
YOU MIGHT STILL BE UPSET THAT YOUR OLD OWNER HAD TO LEAVE QUITE SUDDENLY, BUT I WANT TO REASSURE YOU WE WILL DO EVERYTHING IN OUR POWER TO MAKE YOU FEEL AT HOME
. . . WHY DID YOU HAVE A SHAVING KIT INSIDE YOUR BATHROOM?
A WOLF HAS TO HAVE HIS SECRETS
HEY DARYL! WHY DO YOU HAVE A SHAVING KIT IN OUR BATHROOM?
GOOD MORNING KING
I AM KEENE MILTON YOUR NEW OWNER, THOUGH ≠AHEM≠ DON'T GO AROUND SAYING THAT BECAUSE IT'S TECHNICALLY NOT TRUE FOR THREE SEPARATE LEGAL REASONS
CAN I ASK WHAT HAPPENED? I'M A LITTLE BEHIND
OUR STEWARD GOT A CALL THAT YOUR OWNER, ONE OF OUR RESIDENTS, VANISHED LAST NIGHT
WE THOUGHT FOR A WHILE YOU WENT WITH HIM, BUT THEN THE K-9S FOUND YOU PASSED OUT IN THE WOODS
SO I HAD HIM ADD YOU TO OUR LITTLE PROGRAM
AT LEAST UNTIL YOUR OWNER RETURNS, IF HE DOES
ARE YOU FINE WITH ALL OF THAT?
ACTUALLY, I DO HAVE A SMALL REQUEST IN CASE HE DOES RETURN
WHAT'S THAT?
PLEASE PLEASE PLEASE GRANT ME ASYLUM
FUNNY, MOST OF OUR OTHER PROSPECTS ASKED THE SAME THING
AFTER RUNNING AWAY SCREAMING FROM THIS HOUSE

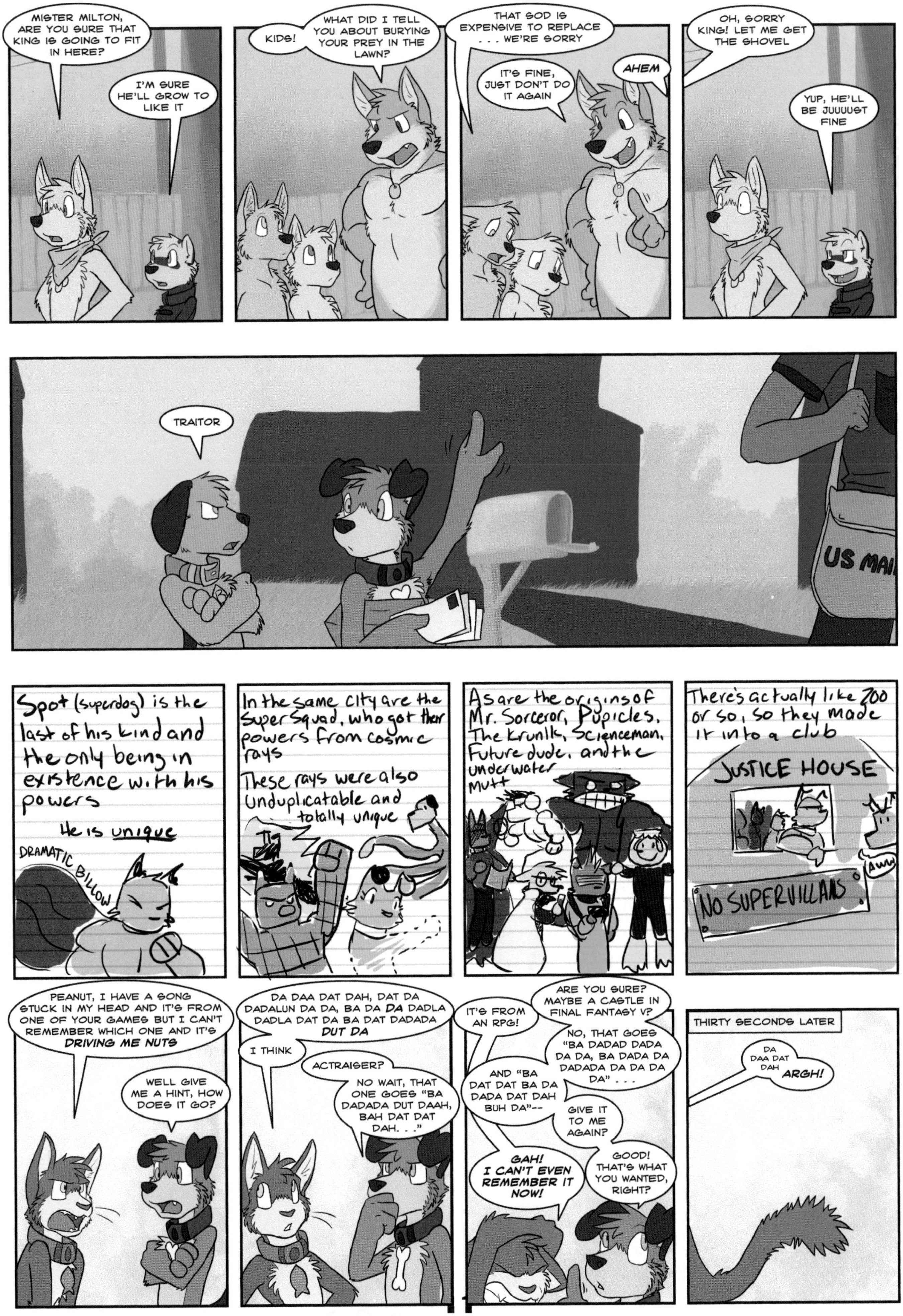
MISTER MILTON, ARE YOU SURE THAT KING IS GOING TO FIT IN HERE?
I'M SURE HE'LL GROW TO LIKE IT
KIDS!
WHAT DID I TELL YOU ABOUT BURYING YOUR PREY IN THE LAWN?
THAT SOD IS EXPENSIVE TO REPLACE . . . WE'RE SORRY
IT'S FINE, JUST DON'T DO IT AGAIN
AHEM
OH, SORRY KING! LET ME GET THE SHOVEL
YUP, HE'LL BE JUUUUST FINE
TRAITOR
US MAI
Spot (superdog) is the last of his kind and the only being in existence with his powers
He is unique
DRAMATIC BILLOW
In the same city are the SuperSquad, who got their powers from cosmic rays
These rays were also unduplicatable and totally unique
As are the origins of Mr. Sorceror, Pupicles, The Krunlk, Scienceman, Future dude, and the underwater mutt
There's actually like 200 or so, so they made it into a club
JUSTICE HOUSE
NO SUPERVILLANS
AWW
PEANUT, I HAVE A SONG STUCK IN MY HEAD AND IT'S FROM ONE OF YOUR GAMES BUT I CAN'T REMEMBER WHICH ONE AND IT'S DRIVING ME NUTS
WELL GIVE ME A HINT, HOW DOES IT GO?
DA DAA DAT DAH, DAT DA DADALUN DA DA, BA DA DA DADLA DADLA DAT DA BA DAT DADADA DUT DA
I THINK
ACTRAISER?
NO WAIT, THAT ONE GOES "BA DADADA DUT DAAH, BAH DAT DAT DAH. . ."
IT'S FROM AN RPG!
ARE YOU SURE? MAYBE A CASTLE IN FINAL FANTASY V?
NO, THAT GOES "BA DADAD DADA DA DA, BA DADA DA DADADA DA DA DA DA" . . .
AND "BA DAT DAT BA DA DADA DAT DAH BUH DA"--
GIVE IT TO ME AGAIN?
GAH! I CAN'T EVEN REMEMBER IT NOW!
GOOD! THAT'S WHAT YOU WANTED, RIGHT?
THIRTY SECONDS LATER
DA DAA DAT DAH ARGH!

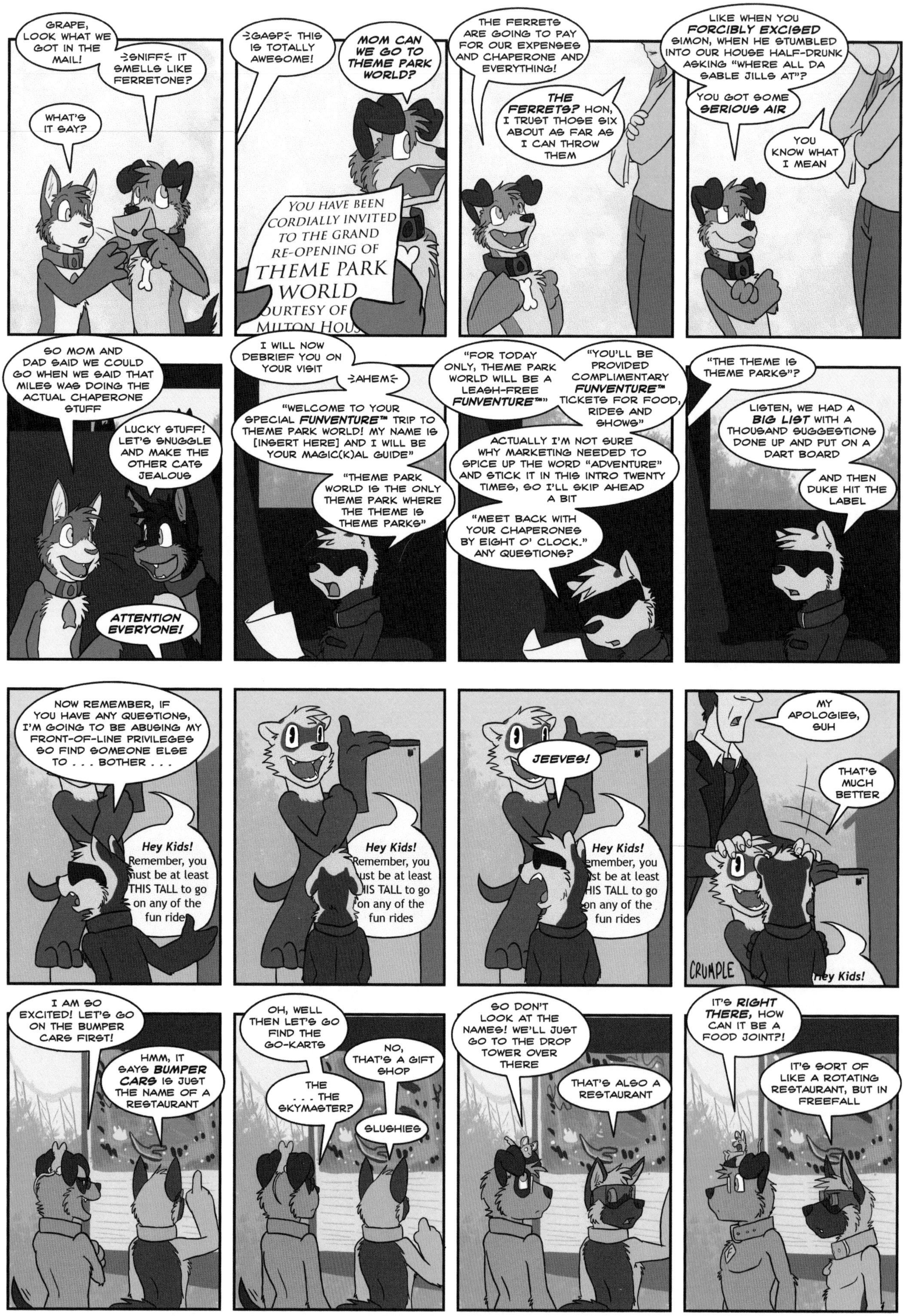
GRAPE, LOOK WHAT WE GOT IN THE MAIL!
⇒SNIFF⇐ IT SMELLS LIKE FERRETONE?
WHAT'S IT SAY?
⇒GASP⇐ THIS IS TOTALLY AWESOME!
MOM CAN WE GO TO THEME PARK WORLD?
YOU HAVE BEEN CORDIALLY INVITED TO THE GRAND RE-OPENING OF THEME PARK WORLD
THE FERRETS ARE GOING TO PAY FOR OUR EXPENSES AND CHAPERONE AND EVERYTHING!
THE FERRETS? HON, I TRUST THOSE SIX ABOUT AS FAR AS I CAN THROW THEM
LIKE WHEN YOU FORCIBLY EXCISED SIMON, WHEN HE STUMBLED INTO OUR HOUSE HALF-DRUNK ASKING "WHERE ALL DA SABLE JILLS AT"?
YOU GOT SOME SERIOUS AIR
YOU KNOW WHAT I MEAN
SO MOM AND DAD SAID WE COULD GO WHEN WE SAID THAT MILES WAS DOING THE ACTUAL CHAPERONE STUFF
LUCKY STUFF! LET'S SNUGGLE AND MAKE THE OTHER CATS JEALOUS
ATTENTION EVERYONE!
I WILL NOW DEBRIEF YOU ON YOUR VISIT
⇒AHEM⇐
"WELCOME TO YOUR SPECIAL FUNVENTURE™ TRIP TO THEME PARK WORLD! MY NAME IS [INSERT HERE] AND I WILL BE YOUR MAGIC(K)AL GUIDE"
"THEME PARK WORLD IS THE ONLY THEME PARK WHERE THE THEME IS THEME PARKS"
"FOR TODAY ONLY, THEME PARK WORLD WILL BE A LEASH-FREE FUNVENTURE™"
"YOU'LL BE PROVIDED COMPLIMENTARY FUNVENTURE™ TICKETS FOR FOOD, RIDES AND SHOWS"
ACTUALLY I'M NOT SURE WHY MARKETING NEEDED TO SPICE UP THE WORD "ADVENTURE" AND STICK IT IN THIS INTRO TWENTY TIMES, SO I'LL SKIP AHEAD A BIT
"MEET BACK WITH YOUR CHAPERONES BY EIGHT O' CLOCK." ANY QUESTIONS?
"THE THEME IS THEME PARKS"?
LISTEN, WE HAD A BIG LIST WITH A THOUSAND SUGGESTIONS DONE UP AND PUT ON A DART BOARD
AND THEN DUKE HIT THE LABEL
NOW REMEMBER, IF YOU HAVE ANY QUESTIONS, I'M GOING TO BE ABUSING MY FRONT-OF-LINE PRIVILEGES SO FIND SOMEONE ELSE TO . . . BOTHER . . .
Hey Kids! Remember, you must be at least THIS TALL to go on any of the fun rides
JEEVES!
MY APOLOGIES, SUH
THAT'S MUCH BETTER
CRUMPLE
Hey Kids!
I AM SO EXCITED! LET'S GO ON THE BUMPER CARS FIRST!
HMM, IT SAYS BUMPER CARS IS JUST THE NAME OF A RESTAURANT
OH, WELL THEN LET'S GO FIND THE GO-KARTS
NO, THAT'S A GIFT SHOP
THE . . . THE SKYMASTER?
SLUSHIES
SO DON'T LOOK AT THE NAMES! WE'LL JUST GO TO THE DROP TOWER OVER THERE
THAT'S ALSO A RESTAURANT
IT'S RIGHT THERE, HOW CAN IT BE A FOOD JOINT?!
IT'S SORT OF LIKE A ROTATING RESTAURANT, BUT IN FREEFALL

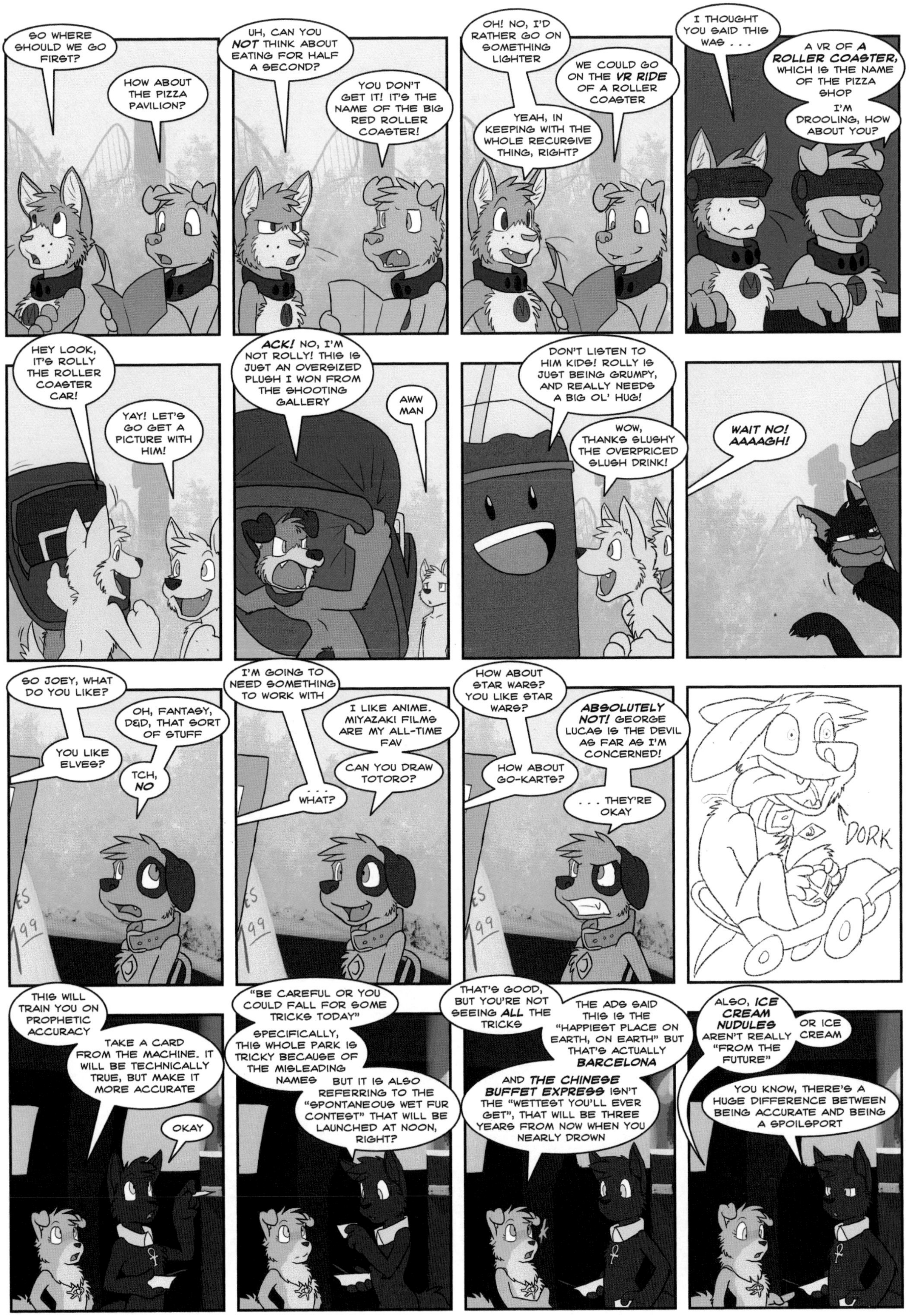
SO WHERE SHOULD WE GO FIRST?
HOW ABOUT THE PIZZA PAVILION?
UH, CAN YOU NOT THINK ABOUT EATING FOR HALF A SECOND?
YOU DON'T GET IT! IT'S THE NAME OF THE BIG RED ROLLER COASTER!
OH! NO, I'D RATHER GO ON SOMETHING LIGHTER
WE COULD GO ON THE VR RIDE OF A ROLLER COASTER
YEAH, IN KEEPING WITH THE WHOLE RECURSIVE THING, RIGHT?
I THOUGHT YOU SAID THIS WAS . . .
A VR OF A ROLLER COASTER, WHICH IS THE NAME OF THE PIZZA SHOP
I'M DROOLING, HOW ABOUT YOU?
HEY LOOK, IT'S ROLLY THE ROLLER COASTER CAR!
YAY! LET'S GO GET A PICTURE WITH HIM!
ACK! NO, I'M NOT ROLLY! THIS IS JUST AN OVERSIZED PLUSH I WON FROM THE SHOOTING GALLERY
AWW MAN
DON'T LISTEN TO HIM KIDS! ROLLY IS JUST BEING GRUMPY, AND REALLY NEEDS A BIG OL' HUG!
WOW, THANKS SLUSHY THE OVERPRICED SLUSH DRINK!
WAIT NO! AAAAGH!
SO JOEY, WHAT DO YOU LIKE?
OH, FANTASY, D&D, THAT SORT OF STUFF
YOU LIKE ELVES?
TCH, NO
I'M GOING TO NEED SOMETHING TO WORK WITH
I LIKE ANIME. MIYAZAKI FILMS ARE MY ALL-TIME FAV
CAN YOU DRAW TOTORO?
. . . WHAT?
HOW ABOUT STAR WARS? YOU LIKE STAR WARS?
ABSOLUTELY NOT! GEORGE LUCAS IS THE DEVIL AS FAR AS I'M CONCERNED!
HOW ABOUT GO-KARTS?
. . . THEY'RE OKAY
DORK
THIS WILL TRAIN YOU ON PROPHETIC ACCURACY
TAKE A CARD FROM THE MACHINE. IT WILL BE TECHNICALLY TRUE, BUT MAKE IT MORE ACCURATE
OKAY
"BE CAREFUL OR YOU COULD FALL FOR SOME TRICKS TODAY"
SPECIFICALLY, THIS WHOLE PARK IS TRICKY BECAUSE OF THE MISLEADING NAMES
BUT IT IS ALSO REFERRING TO THE "SPONTANEOUS WET FUR CONTEST" THAT WILL BE LAUNCHED AT NOON, RIGHT?
THAT'S GOOD, BUT YOU'RE NOT SEEING ALL THE TRICKS
THE ADS SAID THIS IS THE "HAPPIEST PLACE ON EARTH, ON EARTH" BUT THAT'S ACTUALLY BARCELONA
AND THE CHINESE BUFFET EXPRESS ISN'T THE "WETTEST YOU'LL EVER GET", THAT WILL BE THREE YEARS FROM NOW WHEN YOU NEARLY DROWN
ALSO, ICE CREAM NUDULES AREN'T REALLY "FROM THE FUTURE"
OR ICE CREAM
YOU KNOW, THERE'S A HUGE DIFFERENCE BETWEEN BEING ACCURATE AND BEING A SPOILSPORT

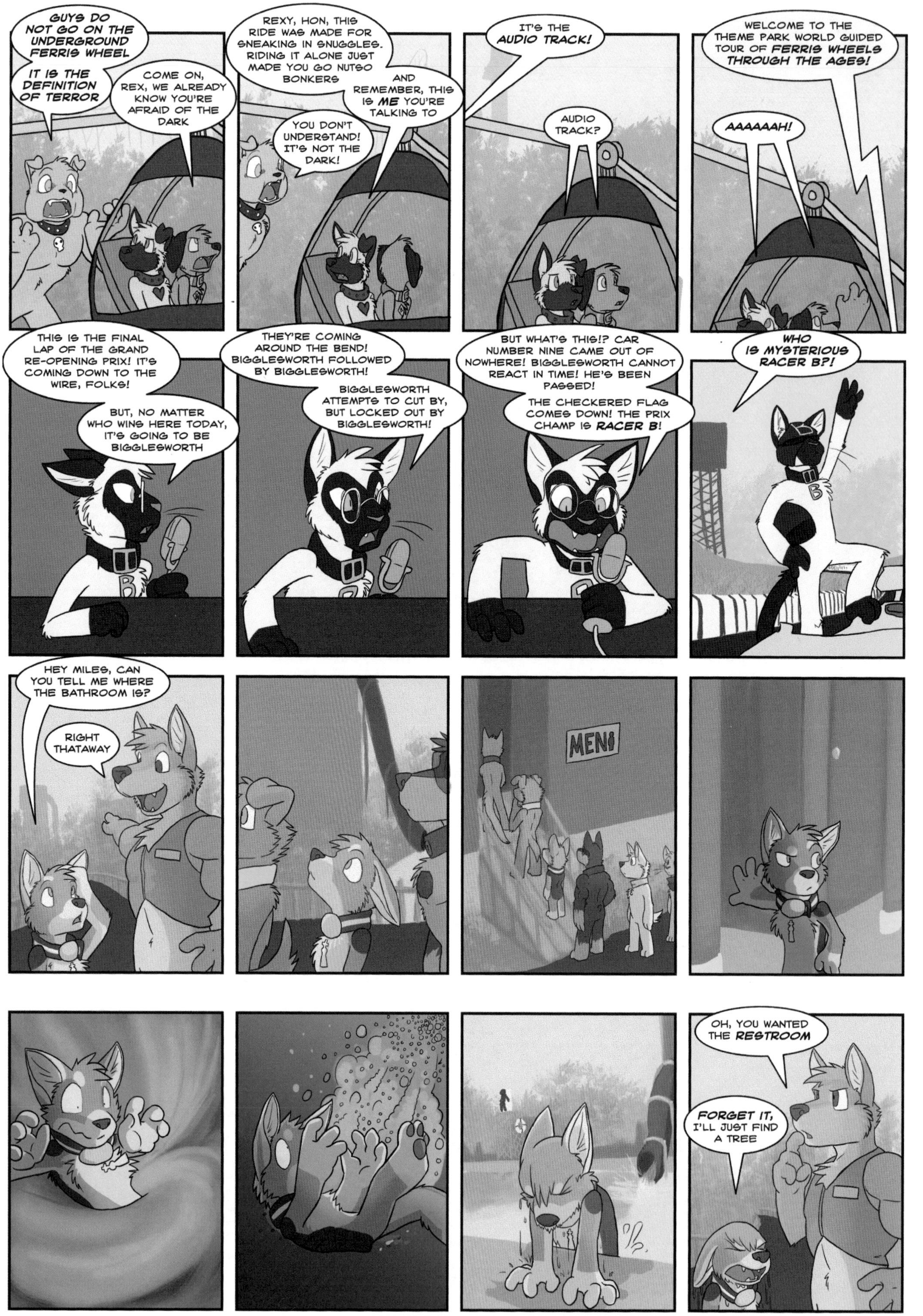
GUYS DO NOT GO ON THE UNDERGROUND FERRIS WHEEL
IT IS THE DEFINITION OF TERROR
COME ON, REX, WE ALREADY KNOW YOU'RE AFRAID OF THE DARK
REXY, HON, THIS RIDE WAS MADE FOR SNEAKING IN SNUGGLES. RIDING IT ALONE JUST MADE YOU GO NUTSO BONKERS
AND REMEMBER, THIS IS ME YOU'RE TALKING TO
YOU DON'T UNDERSTAND! IT'S NOT THE DARK!
IT'S THE AUDIO TRACK!
AUDIO TRACK?
WELCOME TO THE THEME PARK WORLD GUIDED TOUR OF FERRIS WHEELS THROUGH THE AGES!
AAAAAAH!
THIS IS THE FINAL LAP OF THE GRAND RE-OPENING PRIX! IT'S COMING DOWN TO THE WIRE, FOLKS!
BUT, NO MATTER WHO WINS HERE TODAY, IT'S GOING TO BE BIGGLESWORTH
THEY'RE COMING AROUND THE BEND! BIGGLESWORTH FOLLOWED BY BIGGLESWORTH!
BIGGLESWORTH ATTEMPTS TO CUT BY, BUT LOCKED OUT BY BIGGLESWORTH!
BUT WHAT'S THIS!? CAR NUMBER NINE CAME OUT OF NOWHERE! BIGGLESWORTH CANNOT REACT IN TIME! HE'S BEEN PASSED!
THE CHECKERED FLAG COMES DOWN! THE PRIX CHAMP IS RACER B!
WHO IS MYSTERIOUS RACER B?!
HEY MILES, CAN YOU TELL ME WHERE THE BATHROOM IS?
RIGHT THATAWAY
MENS
OH, YOU WANTED THE RESTROOM
FORGET IT, I'LL JUST FIND A TREE

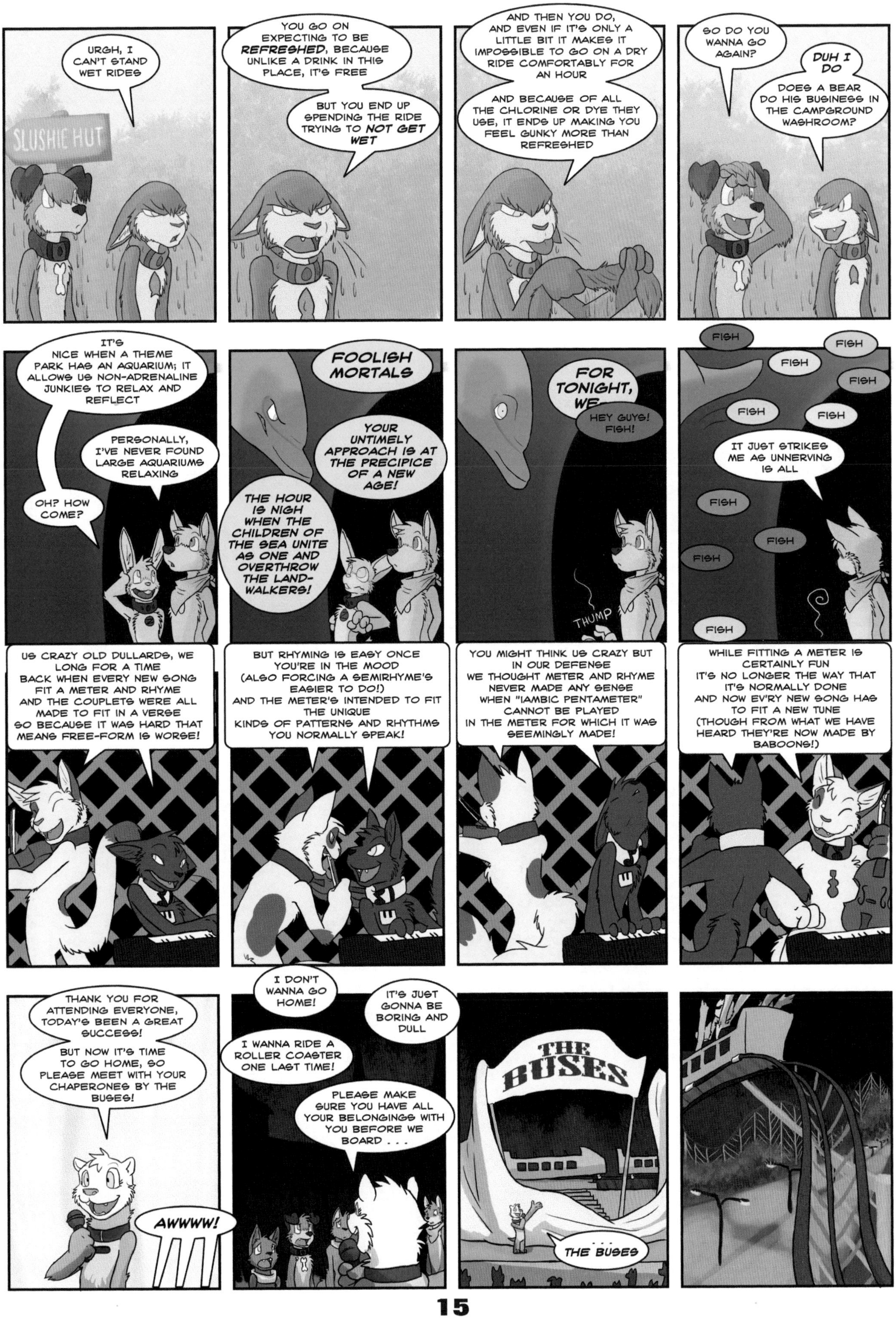
URGH, I CAN'T STAND WET RIDES
SLUSHIE HUT
YOU GO ON EXPECTING TO BE REFRESHED, BECAUSE UNLIKE A DRINK IN THIS PLACE, IT'S FREE
BUT YOU END UP SPENDING THE RIDE TRYING TO NOT GET WET
AND THEN YOU DO, AND EVEN IF IT'S ONLY A LITTLE BIT IT MAKES IT IMPOSSIBLE TO GO ON A DRY RIDE COMFORTABLY FOR AN HOUR
AND BECAUSE OF ALL THE CHLORINE OR DYE THEY USE, IT ENDS UP MAKING YOU FEEL GUNKY MORE THAN REFRESHED
SO DO YOU WANNA GO AGAIN?
DUH I DO
DOES A BEAR DO HIS BUSINESS IN THE CAMPGROUND WASHROOM?
IT'S NICE WHEN A THEME PARK HAS AN AQUARIUM; IT ALLOWS US NON-ADRENALINE JUNKIES TO RELAX AND REFLECT
PERSONALLY, I'VE NEVER FOUND LARGE AQUARIUMS RELAXING
OH? HOW COME?
FOOLISH MORTALS
YOUR UNTIMELY APPROACH IS AT THE PRECIPICE OF A NEW AGE!
THE HOUR IS NIGH WHEN THE CHILDREN OF THE SEA UNITE AS ONE AND OVERTHROW THE LAND-WALKERS!
FOR TONIGHT, WE-
HEY GUYS! FISH!
THUMP
FISH
FISH
FISH
FISH
FISH
FISH
IT JUST STRIKES ME AS UNNERVING IS ALL
FISH
FISH
FISH
FISH
US CRAZY OLD DULLARDS, WE LONG FOR A TIME BACK WHEN EVERY NEW SONG FIT A METER AND RHYME AND THE COUPLETS WERE ALL MADE TO FIT IN A VERSE SO BECAUSE IT WAS HARD THAT MEANS FREE-FORM IS WORSE!
BUT RHYMING IS EASY ONCE YOU'RE IN THE MOOD (ALSO FORCING A SEMIRHYME'S EASIER TO DO!) AND THE METER'S INTENDED TO FIT THE UNIQUE KINDS OF PATTERNS AND RHYTHMS YOU NORMALLY SPEAK!
YOU MIGHT THINK US CRAZY BUT IN OUR DEFENSE WE THOUGHT METER AND RHYME NEVER MADE ANY SENSE WHEN "IAMBIC PENTAMETER" CANNOT BE PLAYED IN THE METER FOR WHICH IT WAS SEEMINGLY MADE!
WHILE FITTING A METER IS CERTAINLY FUN IT'S NO LONGER THE WAY THAT IT'S NORMALLY DONE AND NOW EV'RY NEW SONG HAS TO FIT A NEW TUNE (THOUGH FROM WHAT WE HAVE HEARD THEY'RE NOW MADE BY BABOONS!)
THANK YOU FOR ATTENDING EVERYONE, TODAY'S BEEN A GREAT SUCCESS!
BUT NOW IT'S TIME TO GO HOME, SO PLEASE MEET WITH YOUR CHAPERONES BY THE BUSES!
AWWWW!
I DON'T WANNA GO HOME!
IT'S JUST GONNA BE BORING AND DULL
I WANNA RIDE A ROLLER COASTER ONE LAST TIME!
PLEASE MAKE SURE YOU HAVE ALL YOUR BELONGINGS WITH YOU BEFORE WE BOARD . . .
THE BUSES
. . . THE BUSES

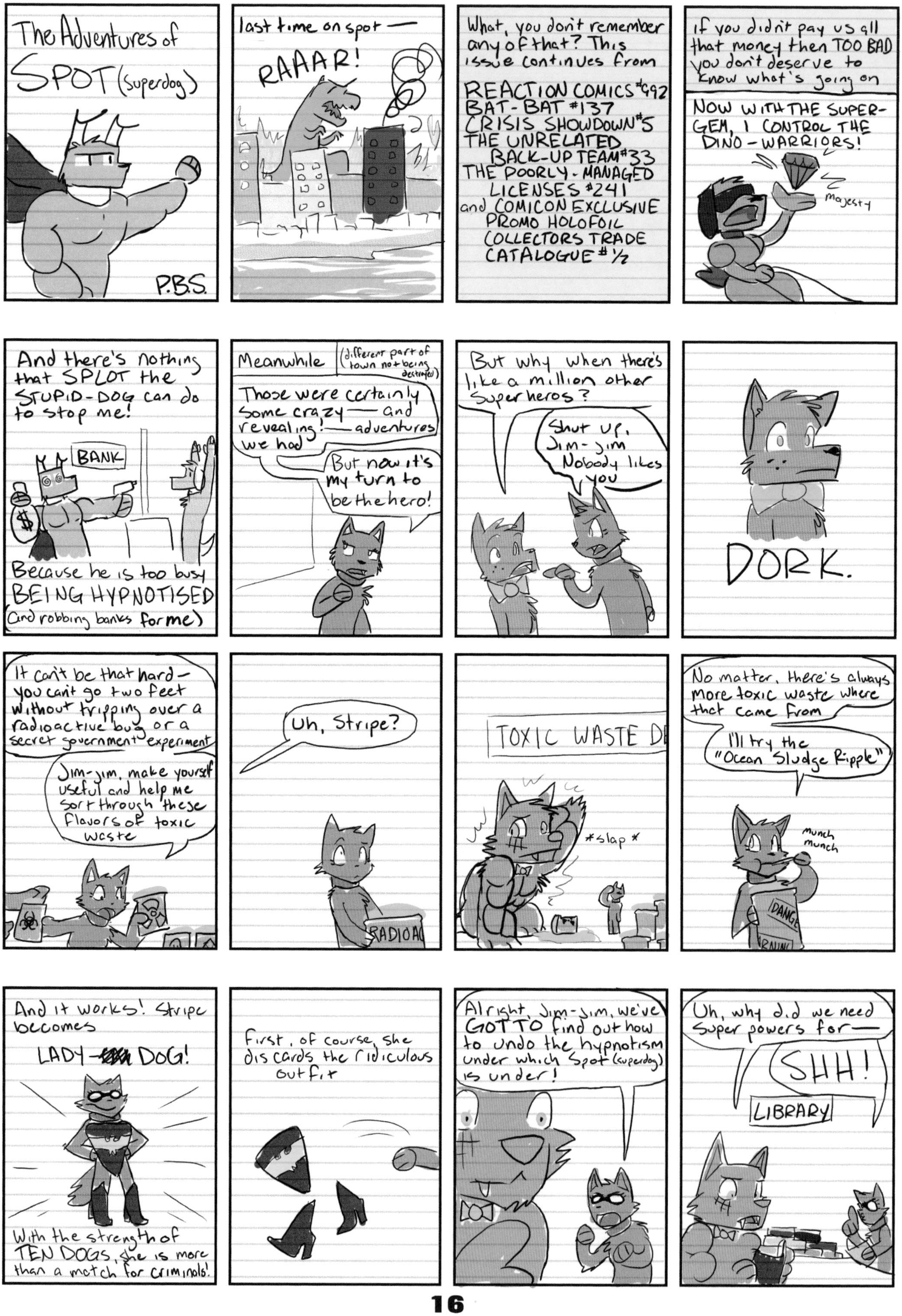

The Adventures of SPOT (superdog)
P.B.S.
last time on spot —
RAAAR!
What, you don't remember any of that? This issue continues from
REACTION COMICS #492
BAT-BAT #137
CRISIS SHOWDOWN #5
THE UNRELATED BACK-UP TEAM #33
THE POORLY-MANAGED LICENSES #241
and COMICON EXCLUSIVE PROMO HOLOFOIL COLLECTORS TRADE CATALOGUE #1/2
If you didn't pay us all that money then TOO BAD you don't deserve to know what's going on
NOW WITH THE SUPER-GEM, I CONTROL THE DINO-WARRIORS!
Majesty
And there's nothing that SPLOT the STUPID-DOG can do to stop me!
BANK
Because he is too busy BEING HYPNOTISED (and robbing banks for me)
Meanwhile
(different part of town not being destroyed)
Those were certainly some crazy — and revealing! — adventures we had
But now it's my turn to be the hero!
But why when there's like a million other Superheros?
Shut up, Jim-jim Nobody likes you
DORK.
It can't be that hard — you can't go two feet without tripping over a radioactive bug or a secret government experiment
Jim-jim, make yourself useful and help me sort through these flavors of toxic waste
Uh, Stripe?
RADIOAC
TOXIC WASTE D
slap
No matter, there's always more toxic waste where that came from
I'll try the "Ocean Sludge Ripple"
munch munch
DANGE
And it works! Stripe becomes
LADY-DOG!
With the strength of TEN DOGS, she is more than a match for criminals!
First, of course, she discards the ridiculous outfit
Alright, Jim-jim, we've GOTTO find out how to undo the hypnotism under which Spot (superdog) is under!
Uh, why did we need super powers for —
SHH!
LIBRARY

Here it is! The hypnotism can only be cured with magic!
Great! All we need to do is find a wizard!
AND BEAT THE SECRET OUT OF HIM
WIZARD CONVENTION
Did you hear about the new SpellNook™?
That sounds like the setup to a bad joke
that's because it is!
DOHOHOHO HOHOHO
AHAHAHAHAHA PREPARE TO EAT IT, WIZARDS!
AAAAH DON'T HURT ME
BROOSH!
Oh you don't understand, we're good guys. we only beat up badguy wizards
Is anyone here a nefarious villain?
no.
Well, does anyone know how to fix hypnosis?
You'll want to go to the panel on hypnosis
HYPNOSIS PANEL
may I have ein volunteer from der audience?
ME! me me me me me
You are getting sleepy... veeery sleepy!
Ven you vake up, you vill know die secrets of breaking der hypnosis
Viggle Viggle
snap
gasp
Ach du lieber! Ich kenne die secrets der hypnosis!
And so they rush to save Spot (superdog)
You already robbed us
Yeah but there's only so many banks in this city
HAHAHAHAHA! PREPARE TO EAT ANTIDOTE, SPOT!
Oh no?
KBROOSH
I'm sorry, but I can't allow you to do that!
hypnosis you see
Ah, but the antidote is...
SNAP
Wait now I forgot what the antidote was
That's okay, now I'm mysteriously better
NEXT... The DINO-WARRIORS?

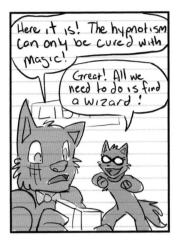

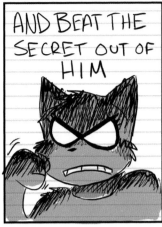

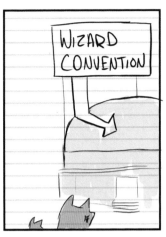

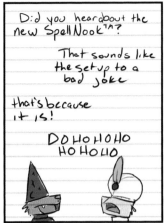

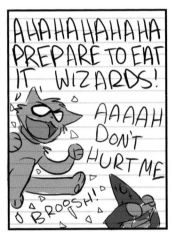

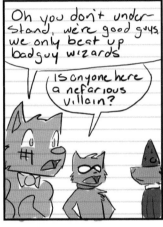

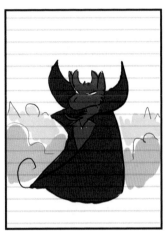

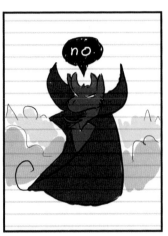

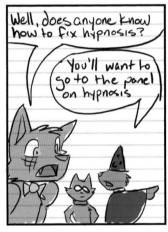

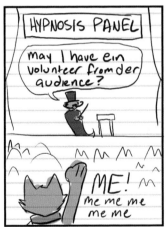

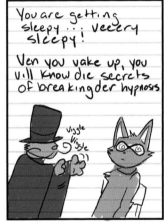

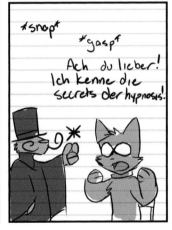

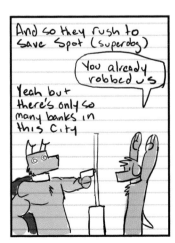

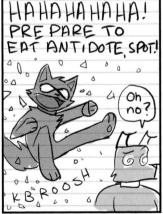

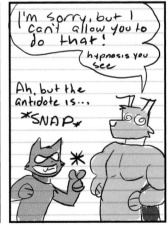

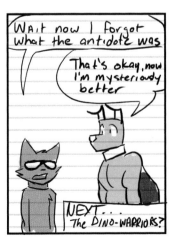

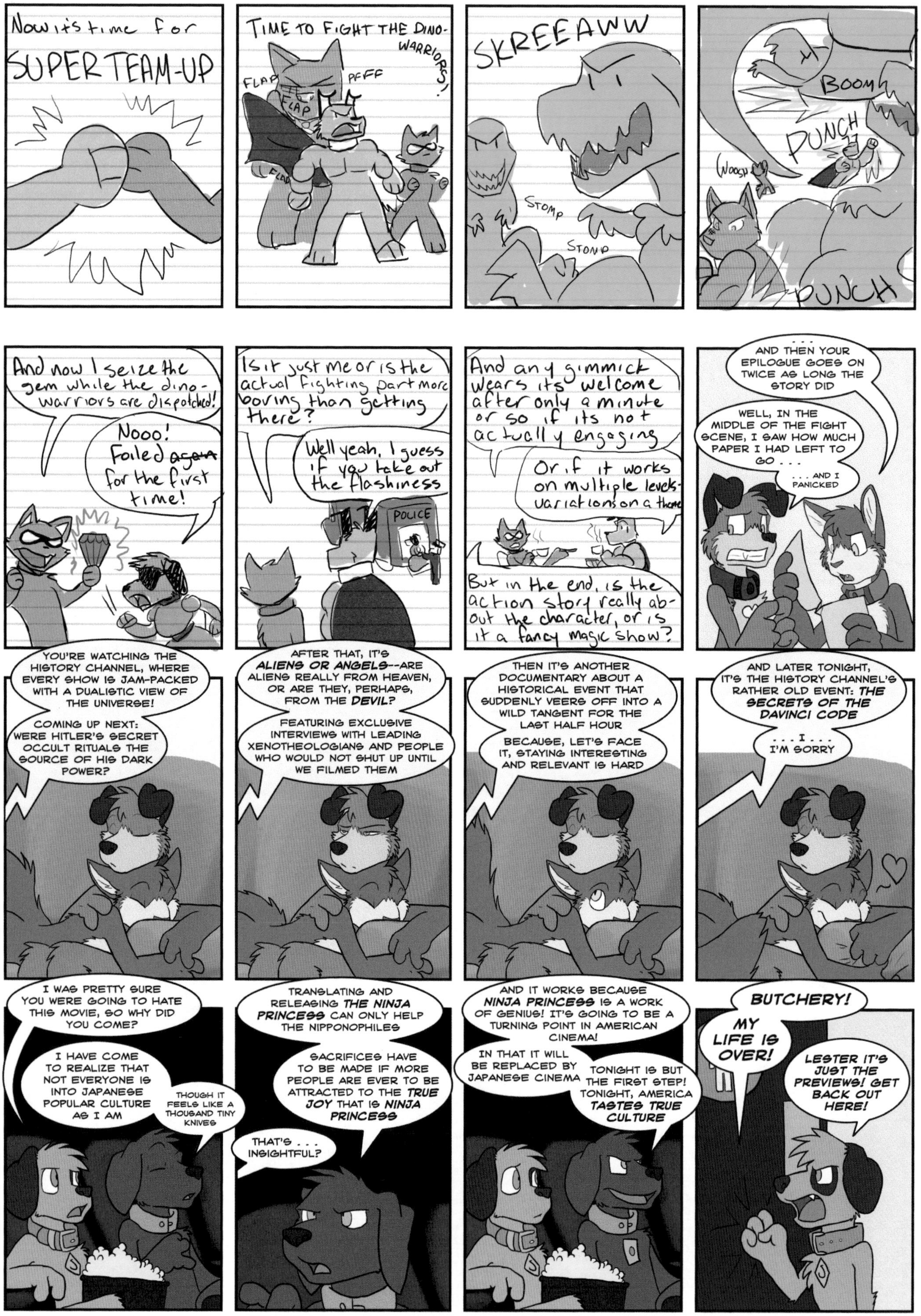

Now it's time for
SUPER TEAM-UP
TIME TO FIGHT THE DINO-WARRIORS!
FLAP
FLAP
PFFF
FLAP
SKREEAWW
STOMP
STOMP
BOOM
PUNCH
WOOSH
PUNCH
And now I seize the gem while the dino-warriors are dispatched!
Nooo! Foiled ~~again~~ for the first time!
Is it just me or is the actual fighting part more boring than getting there?
Well yeah, I guess if you take out the flashiness
POLICE
And any gimmick wears its welcome after only a minute or so if its not actually engaging
Or if it works on multiple levels- variations on a theme
But in the end, is the action story really about the character, or is it a fancy magic show?
. . . AND THEN YOUR EPILOGUE GOES ON TWICE AS LONG THE STORY DID
WELL, IN THE MIDDLE OF THE FIGHT SCENE, I SAW HOW MUCH PAPER I HAD LEFT TO GO . . .
. . . AND I PANICKED
YOU'RE WATCHING THE HISTORY CHANNEL, WHERE EVERY SHOW IS JAM-PACKED WITH A DUALISTIC VIEW OF THE UNIVERSE!
COMING UP NEXT: WERE HITLER'S SECRET OCCULT RITUALS THE SOURCE OF HIS DARK POWER?
AFTER THAT, IT'S ***ALIENS OR ANGELS***--ARE ALIENS REALLY FROM HEAVEN, OR ARE THEY, PERHAPS, FROM THE ***DEVIL?***
FEATURING EXCLUSIVE INTERVIEWS WITH LEADING XENOTHEOLOGIANS AND PEOPLE WHO WOULD NOT SHUT UP UNTIL WE FILMED THEM
THEN IT'S ANOTHER DOCUMENTARY ABOUT A HISTORICAL EVENT THAT SUDDENLY VEERS OFF INTO A WILD TANGENT FOR THE LAST HALF HOUR
BECAUSE, LET'S FACE IT, STAYING INTERESTING AND RELEVANT IS HARD
AND LATER TONIGHT, IT'S THE HISTORY CHANNEL'S RATHER OLD EVENT: ***THE SECRETS OF THE DAVINCI CODE***
. . . I . . . I'M SORRY
I WAS PRETTY SURE YOU WERE GOING TO HATE THIS MOVIE, SO WHY DID YOU COME?
I HAVE COME TO REALIZE THAT NOT EVERYONE IS INTO JAPANESE POPULAR CULTURE AS I AM
THOUGH IT FEELS LIKE A THOUSAND TINY KNIVES
TRANSLATING AND RELEASING ***THE NINJA PRINCESS*** CAN ONLY HELP THE NIPPONOPHILES
SACRIFICES HAVE TO BE MADE IF MORE PEOPLE ARE EVER TO BE ATTRACTED TO THE ***TRUE JOY*** THAT IS ***NINJA PRINCESS***
THAT'S . . . INSIGHTFUL?
AND IT WORKS BECAUSE ***NINJA PRINCESS*** IS A WORK OF GENIUS! IT'S GOING TO BE A TURNING POINT IN AMERICAN CINEMA!
IN THAT IT WILL BE REPLACED BY JAPANESE CINEMA
TONIGHT IS BUT THE FIRST STEP! TONIGHT, AMERICA ***TASTES TRUE CULTURE***
BUTCHERY!
MY LIFE IS OVER!
LESTER IT'S JUST THE PREVIEWS! GET BACK OUT HERE!

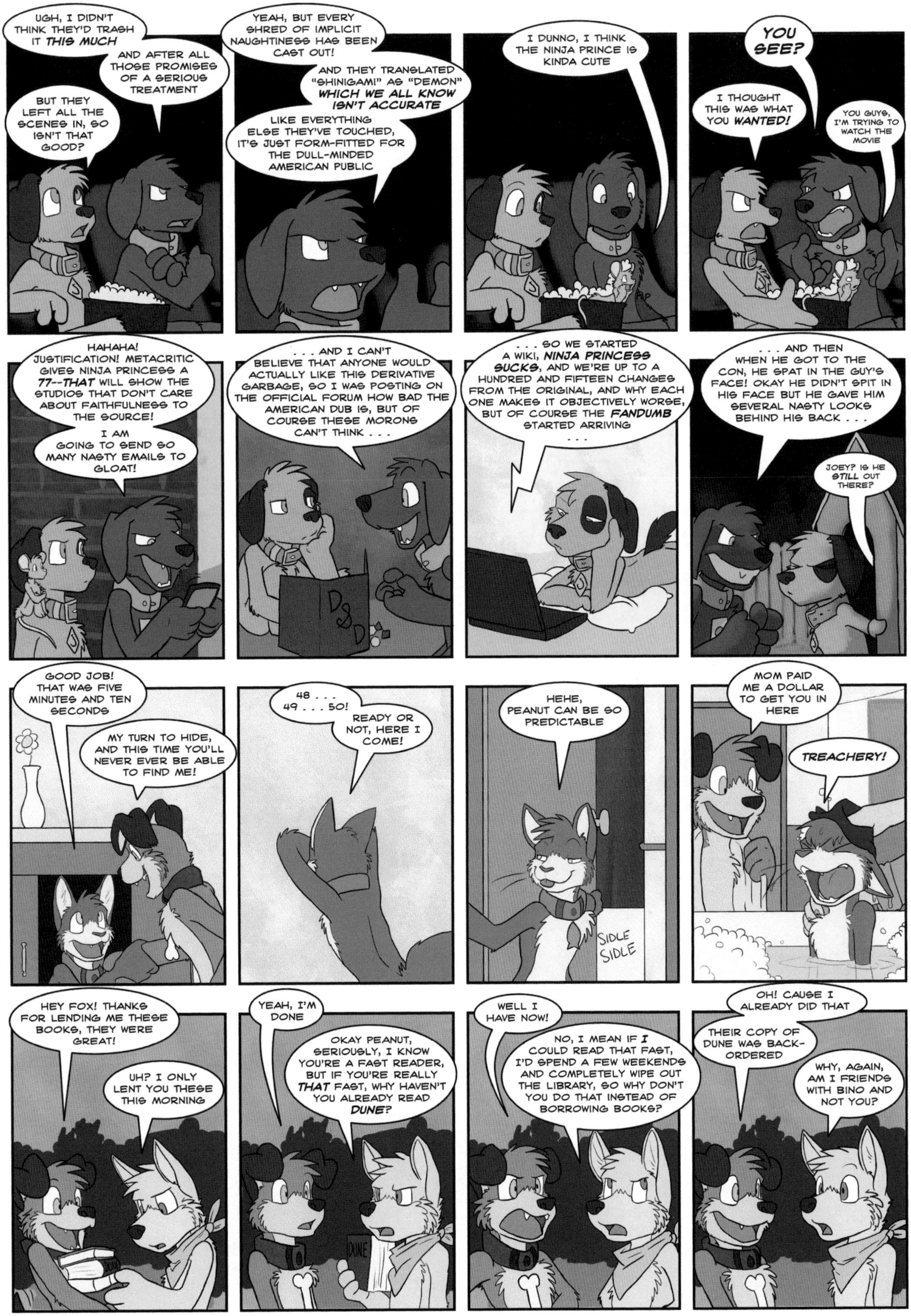
UGH, I DIDN'T THINK THEY'D TRASH IT THIS MUCH
AND AFTER ALL THOSE PROMISES OF A SERIOUS TREATMENT
BUT THEY LEFT ALL THE SCENES IN, SO ISN'T THAT GOOD?
YEAH, BUT EVERY SHRED OF IMPLICIT NAUGHTINESS HAS BEEN CAST OUT!
AND THEY TRANSLATED "SHINIGAMI" AS "DEMON" WHICH WE ALL KNOW ISN'T ACCURATE
LIKE EVERYTHING ELSE THEY'VE TOUCHED, IT'S JUST FORM-FITTED FOR THE DULL-MINDED AMERICAN PUBLIC
I DUNNO, I THINK THE NINJA PRINCE IS KINDA CUTE
YOU SEE?
I THOUGHT THIS WAS WHAT YOU WANTED!
YOU GUYS, I'M TRYING TO WATCH THE MOVIE
HAHAHA! JUSTIFICATION! METACRITIC GIVES NINJA PRINCESS A 77--THAT WILL SHOW THE STUDIOS THAT DON'T CARE ABOUT FAITHFULNESS TO THE SOURCE!
I AM GOING TO SEND SO MANY NASTY EMAILS TO GLOAT!
. . . AND I CAN'T BELIEVE THAT ANYONE WOULD ACTUALLY LIKE THIS DERIVATIVE GARBAGE, SO I WAS POSTING ON THE OFFICIAL FORUM HOW BAD THE AMERICAN DUB IS, BUT OF COURSE THESE MORONS CAN'T THINK . . .
D&D
. . . SO WE STARTED A WIKI, NINJA PRINCESS SUCKS, AND WE'RE UP TO A HUNDRED AND FIFTEEN CHANGES FROM THE ORIGINAL, AND WHY EACH ONE MAKES IT OBJECTIVELY WORSE, BUT OF COURSE THE FANDUMB STARTED ARRIVING . . .
. . . AND THEN WHEN HE GOT TO THE CON, HE SPAT IN THE GUY'S FACE! OKAY HE DIDN'T SPIT IN HIS FACE BUT HE GAVE HIM SEVERAL NASTY LOOKS BEHIND HIS BACK . . .
JOEY? IS HE STILL OUT THERE?
GOOD JOB! THAT WAS FIVE MINUTES AND TEN SECONDS
MY TURN TO HIDE, AND THIS TIME YOU'LL NEVER EVER BE ABLE TO FIND ME!
48 . . . 49 . . . 50!
READY OR NOT, HERE I COME!
HEHE, PEANUT CAN BE SO PREDICTABLE
SIDLE SIDLE
MOM PAID ME A DOLLAR TO GET YOU IN HERE
TREACHERY!
HEY FOX! THANKS FOR LENDING ME THESE BOOKS, THEY WERE GREAT!
UH? I ONLY LENT YOU THESE THIS MORNING
YEAH, I'M DONE
OKAY PEANUT, SERIOUSLY, I KNOW YOU'RE A FAST READER, BUT IF YOU'RE REALLY THAT FAST, WHY HAVEN'T YOU ALREADY READ DUNE?
DUNE
WELL I HAVE NOW!
NO, I MEAN IF I COULD READ THAT FAST, I'D SPEND A FEW WEEKENDS AND COMPLETELY WIPE OUT THE LIBRARY, SO WHY DON'T YOU DO THAT INSTEAD OF BORROWING BOOKS?
OH! CAUSE I ALREADY DID THAT
THEIR COPY OF DUNE WAS BACK-ORDERED
WHY, AGAIN, AM I FRIENDS WITH BINO AND NOT YOU?

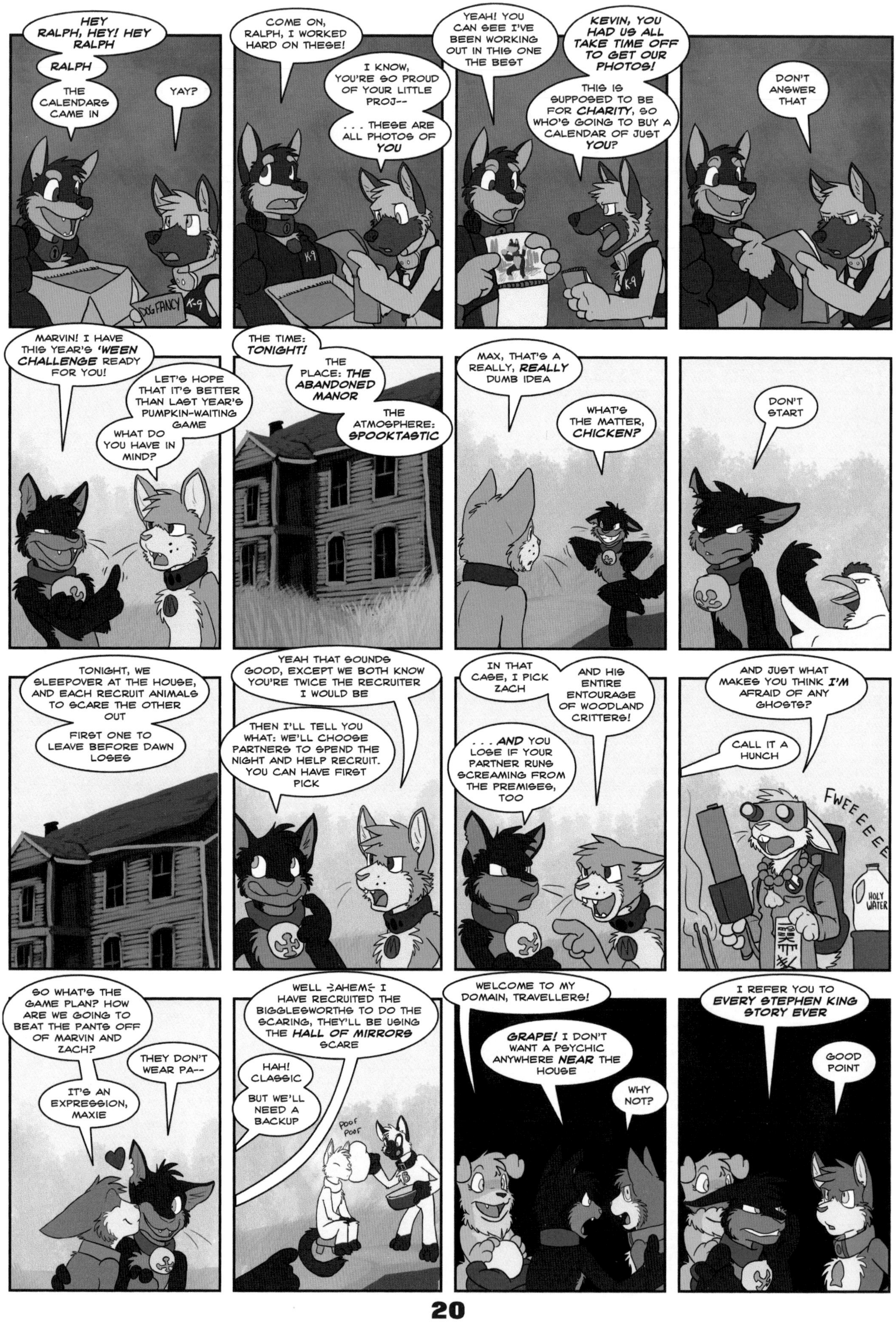
HEY RALPH, HEY! HEY RALPH
RALPH
THE CALENDARS CAME IN
YAY?
DOG FANCY
K-9
COME ON, RALPH, I WORKED HARD ON THESE!
I KNOW, YOU'RE SO PROUD OF YOUR LITTLE PROJ--
. . . THESE ARE ALL PHOTOS OF YOU
K-9
YEAH! YOU CAN SEE I'VE BEEN WORKING OUT IN THIS ONE THE BEST
KEVIN, YOU HAD US ALL TAKE TIME OFF TO GET OUR PHOTOS!
THIS IS SUPPOSED TO BE FOR CHARITY, SO WHO'S GOING TO BUY A CALENDAR OF JUST YOU?
K-9
DON'T ANSWER THAT
MARVIN! I HAVE THIS YEAR'S 'WEEN CHALLENGE READY FOR YOU!
LET'S HOPE THAT IT'S BETTER THAN LAST YEAR'S PUMPKIN-WAITING GAME
WHAT DO YOU HAVE IN MIND?
THE TIME: TONIGHT!
THE PLACE: THE ABANDONED MANOR
THE ATMOSPHERE: SPOOKTASTIC
MAX, THAT'S A REALLY, REALLY DUMB IDEA
WHAT'S THE MATTER, CHICKEN?
DON'T START
TONIGHT, WE SLEEPOVER AT THE HOUSE, AND EACH RECRUIT ANIMALS TO SCARE THE OTHER OUT
FIRST ONE TO LEAVE BEFORE DAWN LOSES
YEAH THAT SOUNDS GOOD, EXCEPT WE BOTH KNOW YOU'RE TWICE THE RECRUITER I WOULD BE
THEN I'LL TELL YOU WHAT: WE'LL CHOOSE PARTNERS TO SPEND THE NIGHT AND HELP RECRUIT. YOU CAN HAVE FIRST PICK
IN THAT CASE, I PICK ZACH
AND HIS ENTIRE ENTOURAGE OF WOODLAND CRITTERS!
. . . AND YOU LOSE IF YOUR PARTNER RUNS SCREAMING FROM THE PREMISES, TOO
AND JUST WHAT MAKES YOU THINK I'M AFRAID OF ANY GHOSTS?
CALL IT A HUNCH
FWEEEEEEE
HOLY WATER
SO WHAT'S THE GAME PLAN? HOW ARE WE GOING TO BEAT THE PANTS OFF OF MARVIN AND ZACH?
THEY DON'T WEAR PA--
IT'S AN EXPRESSION, MAXIE
WELL *AHEM* I HAVE RECRUITED THE BIGGLESWORTHS TO DO THE SCARING, THEY'LL BE USING THE HALL OF MIRRORS SCARE
HAH! CLASSIC
BUT WE'LL NEED A BACKUP
POOF POOF
WELCOME TO MY DOMAIN, TRAVELLERS!
GRAPE! I DON'T WANT A PSYCHIC ANYWHERE NEAR THE HOUSE
WHY NOT?
I REFER YOU TO EVERY STEPHEN KING STORY EVER
GOOD POINT

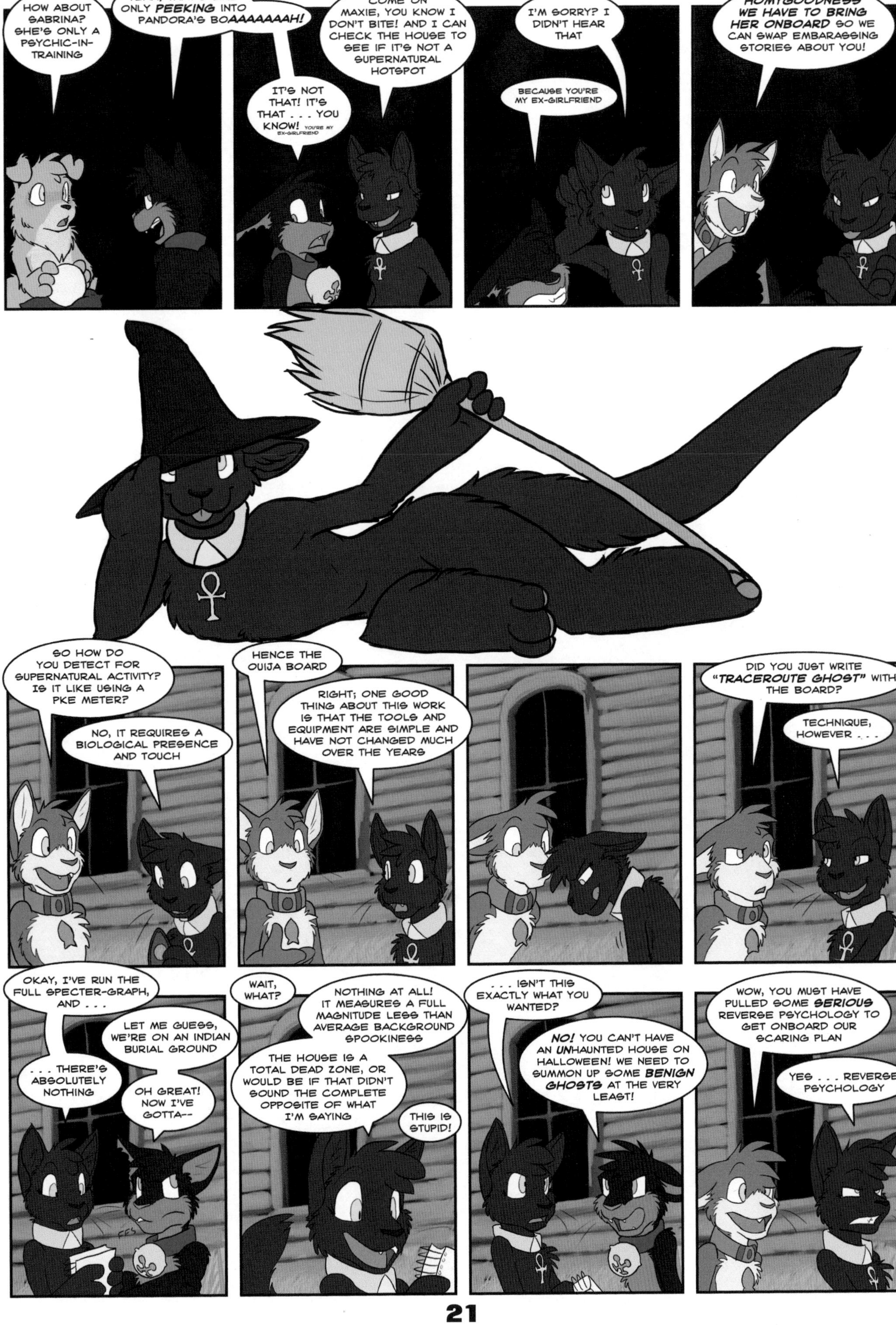
HOW ABOUT SABRINA? SHE'S ONLY A PSYCHIC-IN-TRAINING
YEAH, THAT'S LIKE ONLY PEEKING INTO PANDORA'S BOAAAAAAAH!
COME ON MAXIE, YOU KNOW I DON'T BITE! AND I CAN CHECK THE HOUSE TO SEE IF IT'S NOT A SUPERNATURAL HOTSPOT
IT'S NOT THAT! IT'S THAT . . . YOU KNOW! YOU'RE MY EX-GIRLFRIEND
I'M SORRY? I DIDN'T HEAR THAT
BECAUSE YOU'RE MY EX-GIRLFRIEND
HOMYGOODNESS WE HAVE TO BRING HER ONBOARD SO WE CAN SWAP EMBARASSING STORIES ABOUT YOU!
SO HOW DO YOU DETECT FOR SUPERNATURAL ACTIVITY? IS IT LIKE USING A PKE METER?
NO, IT REQUIRES A BIOLOGICAL PRESENCE AND TOUCH
HENCE THE OUIJA BOARD
RIGHT; ONE GOOD THING ABOUT THIS WORK IS THAT THE TOOLS AND EQUIPMENT ARE SIMPLE AND HAVE NOT CHANGED MUCH OVER THE YEARS
DID YOU JUST WRITE "TRACEROUTE GHOST" WITH THE BOARD?
TECHNIQUE, HOWEVER . . .
OKAY, I'VE RUN THE FULL SPECTER-GRAPH, AND . . .
LET ME GUESS, WE'RE ON AN INDIAN BURIAL GROUND
. . . THERE'S ABSOLUTELY NOTHING
OH GREAT! NOW I'VE GOTTA--
WAIT, WHAT?
NOTHING AT ALL! IT MEASURES A FULL MAGNITUDE LESS THAN AVERAGE BACKGROUND SPOOKINESS
THE HOUSE IS A TOTAL DEAD ZONE, OR WOULD BE IF THAT DIDN'T SOUND THE COMPLETE OPPOSITE OF WHAT I'M SAYING
THIS IS STUPID!
. . . ISN'T THIS EXACTLY WHAT YOU WANTED?
NO! YOU CAN'T HAVE AN UNHAUNTED HOUSE ON HALLOWEEN! WE NEED TO SUMMON UP SOME BENIGN GHOSTS AT THE VERY LEAST!
WOW, YOU MUST HAVE PULLED SOME SERIOUS REVERSE PSYCHOLOGY TO GET ONBOARD OUR SCARING PLAN
YES . . . REVERSE PSYCHOLOGY

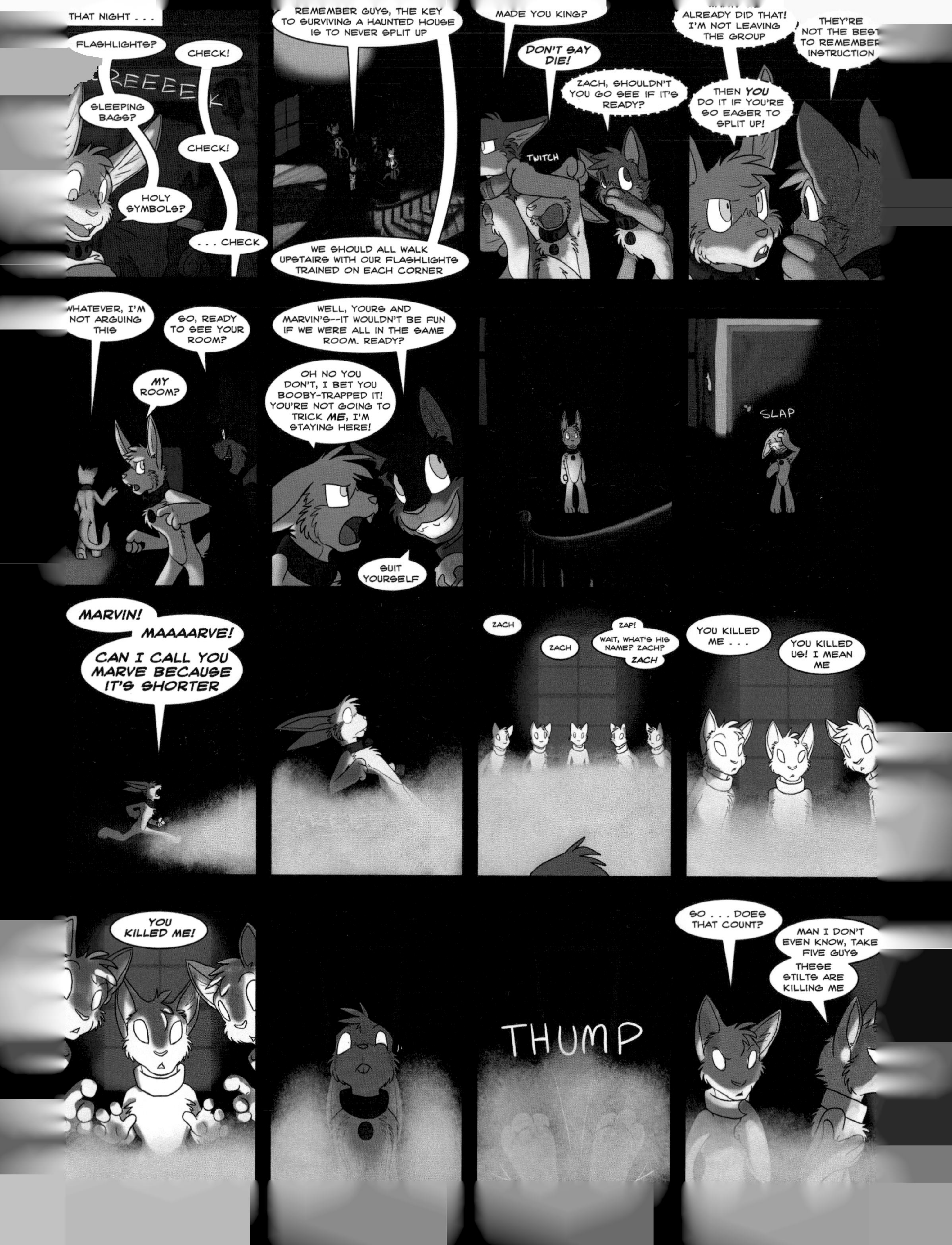

THAT NIGHT . . .
FLASHLIGHTS?
CHECK!
SLEEPING BAGS?
CHECK!
HOLY SYMBOLS?
. . . CHECK
REMEMBER GUYS, THE KEY TO SURVIVING A HAUNTED HOUSE IS TO NEVER SPLIT UP
WE SHOULD ALL WALK UPSTAIRS WITH OUR FLASHLIGHTS TRAINED ON EACH CORNER
MADE YOU KING?
DON'T SAY DIE!
ZACH, SHOULDN'T YOU GO SEE IF IT'S READY?
TWITCH
ALREADY DID THAT! I'M NOT LEAVING THE GROUP
THEY'RE NOT THE BES
TO REMEMBE
INSTRUCTION
THEN YOU DO IT IF YOU'RE SO EAGER TO SPLIT UP!
WHATEVER, I'M NOT ARGUING THIS
SO, READY TO SEE YOUR ROOM?
MY ROOM?
WELL, YOURS AND MARVIN'S--IT WOULDN'T BE FUN IF WE WERE ALL IN THE SAME ROOM. READY?
OH NO YOU DON'T, I BET YOU BOOBY-TRAPPED IT! YOU'RE NOT GOING TO TRICK ME, I'M STAYING HERE!
SUIT YOURSELF
SLAP
MARVIN!
MAAAARVE!
CAN I CALL YOU MARVE BECAUSE IT'S SHORTER
ZACH
ZACH
ZAP!
WAIT, WHAT'S HIS NAME? ZACH?
ZACH
YOU KILLED ME . . .
YOU KILLED US! I MEAN ME
YOU KILLED ME!
THUMP
SO . . . DOES THAT COUNT?
MAN I DON'T EVEN KNOW, TAKE FIVE GUYS
THESE STILTS ARE KILLING ME

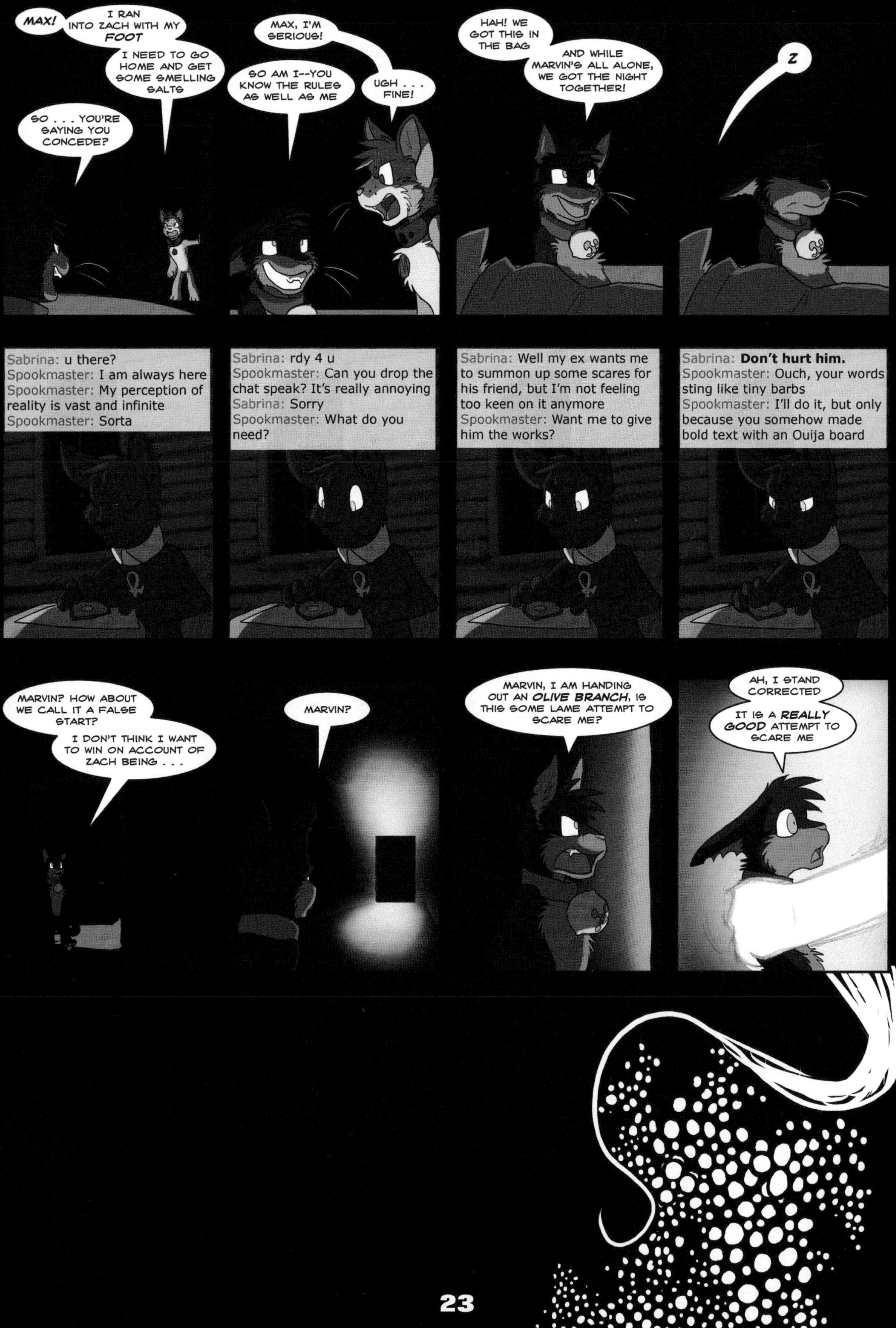
MAX!
I RAN INTO ZACH WITH MY FOOT
I NEED TO GO HOME AND GET SOME SMELLING SALTS
SO . . . YOU'RE SAYING YOU CONCEDE?
MAX, I'M SERIOUS!
SO AM I--YOU KNOW THE RULES AS WELL AS ME
UGH . . . FINE!
HAH! WE GOT THIS IN THE BAG
AND WHILE MARVIN'S ALL ALONE, WE GOT THE NIGHT TOGETHER!
Z
Sabrina: u there?
Spookmaster: I am always here
Spookmaster: My perception of reality is vast and infinite
Spookmaster: Sorta
Sabrina: rdy 4 u
Spookmaster: Can you drop the chat speak? It's really annoying
Sabrina: Sorry
Spookmaster: What do you need?
Sabrina: Well my ex wants me to summon up some scares for his friend, but I'm not feeling too keen on it anymore
Spookmaster: Want me to give him the works?
Sabrina: Don't hurt him.
Spookmaster: Ouch, your words sting like tiny barbs
Spookmaster: I'll do it, but only because you somehow made bold text with an Ouija board
MARVIN? HOW ABOUT WE CALL IT A FALSE START?
I DON'T THINK I WANT TO WIN ON ACCOUNT OF ZACH BEING . . .
MARVIN?
MARVIN, I AM HANDING OUT AN OLIVE BRANCH, IS THIS SOME LAME ATTEMPT TO SCARE ME?
AH, I STAND CORRECTED
IT IS A REALLY GOOD ATTEMPT TO SCARE ME

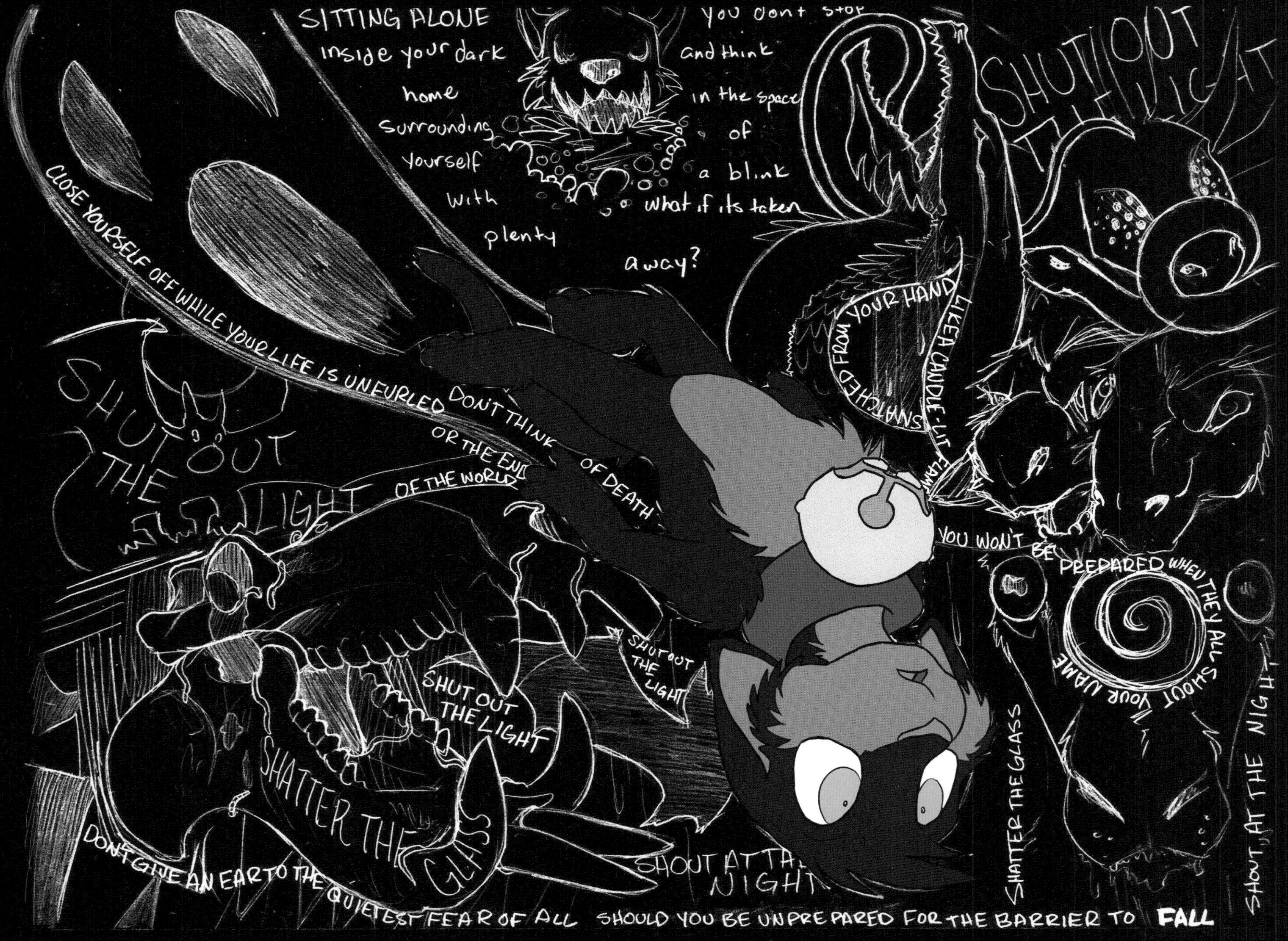
SITTING ALONE
inside your dark
home
surrounding
yourself
with
plenty
you dont stop
and think
in the space
of
a blink
what if its taken
away?
SHUT OUT THE LIGHT
SNATCHED FROM YOUR HAND
LIKE A CANDLE-LIT FLAME
CLOSE YOURSELF OFF WHILE YOUR LIFE IS UNFURLED
DON'T THINK OF DEATH
OR THE END
OF THE WORLD
SHUT OUT THE LIGHT
YOU WON'T BE PREPARED WHEN THEY ALL SHOUT YOUR NAME
SHUT OUT THE LIGHT
SHUT OUT THE LIGHT
SHATTER THE GLASS
SHATTER THE GLASS
SHOUT AT THE NIGHT
SHOUT AT THE NIGHT
DON'T GIVE AN EAR TO THE QUIETEST FEAR OF ALL
SHOULD YOU BE UNPREPARED FOR THE BARRIER TO FALL

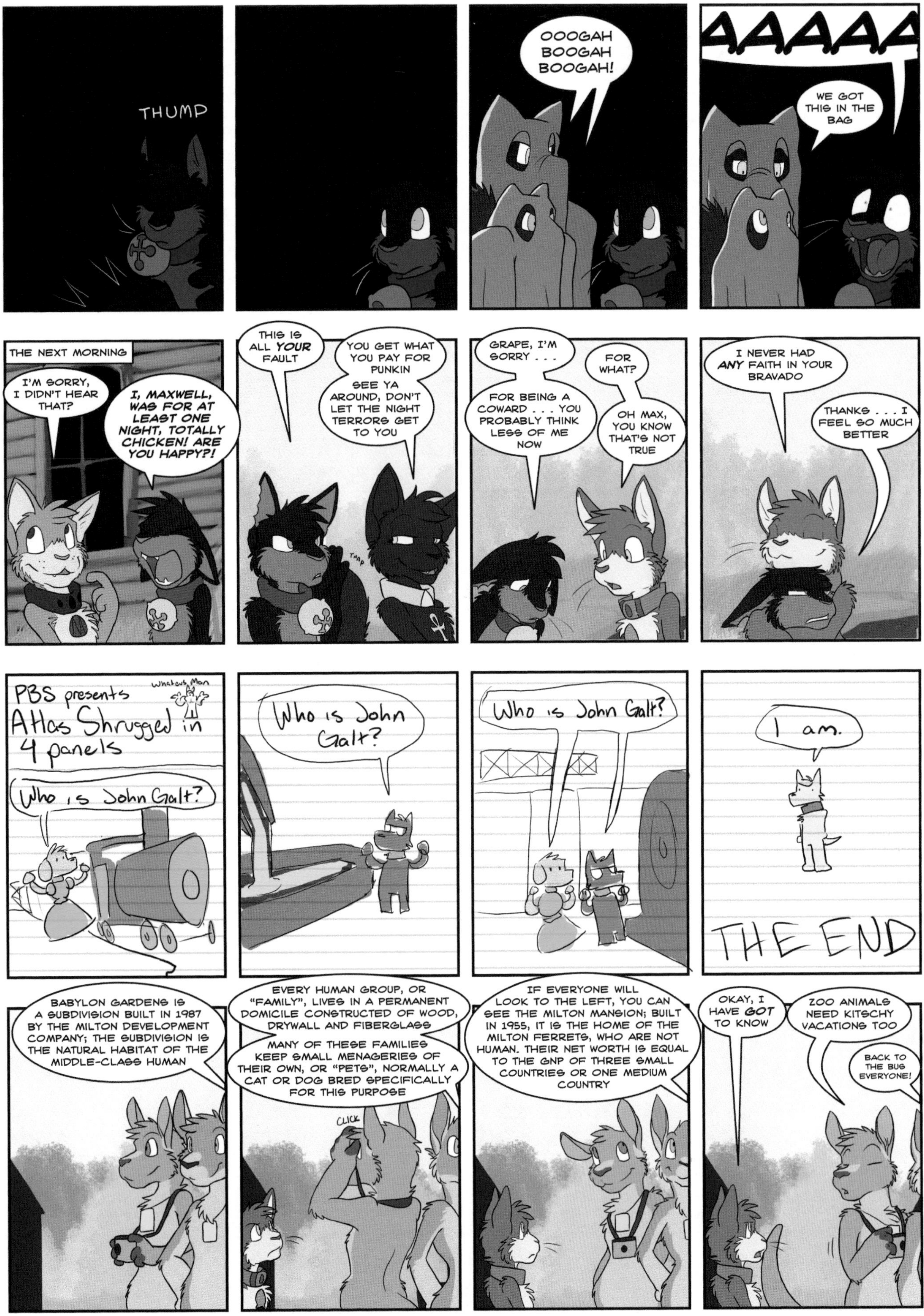
THUMP
OOOGAH BOOGAH BOOGAH!
AAAAA
WE GOT THIS IN THE BAG
THE NEXT MORNING
I'M SORRY, I DIDN'T HEAR THAT?
I, MAXWELL, WAS FOR AT LEAST ONE NIGHT, TOTALLY CHICKEN! ARE YOU HAPPY?!
THIS IS ALL YOUR FAULT
YOU GET WHAT YOU PAY FOR PUNKIN
SEE YA AROUND, DON'T LET THE NIGHT TERRORS GET TO YOU
GRAPE, I'M SORRY . . .
FOR WHAT?
FOR BEING A COWARD . . . YOU PROBABLY THINK LESS OF ME NOW
OH MAX, YOU KNOW THAT'S NOT TRUE
I NEVER HAD ANY FAITH IN YOUR BRAVADO
THANKS . . . I FEEL SO MUCH BETTER
PBS presents
Atlas Shrugged in 4 panels
Who is John Galt?
Who is John Galt?
Who is John Galt?
I am.
THE END
BABYLON GARDENS IS A SUBDIVISION BUILT IN 1987 BY THE MILTON DEVELOPMENT COMPANY; THE SUBDIVISION IS THE NATURAL HABITAT OF THE MIDDLE-CLASS HUMAN
EVERY HUMAN GROUP, OR "FAMILY", LIVES IN A PERMANENT DOMICILE CONSTRUCTED OF WOOD, DRYWALL AND FIBERGLASS
MANY OF THESE FAMILIES KEEP SMALL MENAGERIES OF THEIR OWN, OR "PETS", NORMALLY A CAT OR DOG BRED SPECIFICALLY FOR THIS PURPOSE
CLICK
IF EVERYONE WILL LOOK TO THE LEFT, YOU CAN SEE THE MILTON MANSION; BUILT IN 1955, IT IS THE HOME OF THE MILTON FERRETS, WHO ARE NOT HUMAN. THEIR NET WORTH IS EQUAL TO THE GNP OF THREE SMALL COUNTRIES OR ONE MEDIUM COUNTRY
OKAY, I HAVE GOT TO KNOW
ZOO ANIMALS NEED KITSCHY VACATIONS TOO
BACK TO THE BUS EVERYONE!

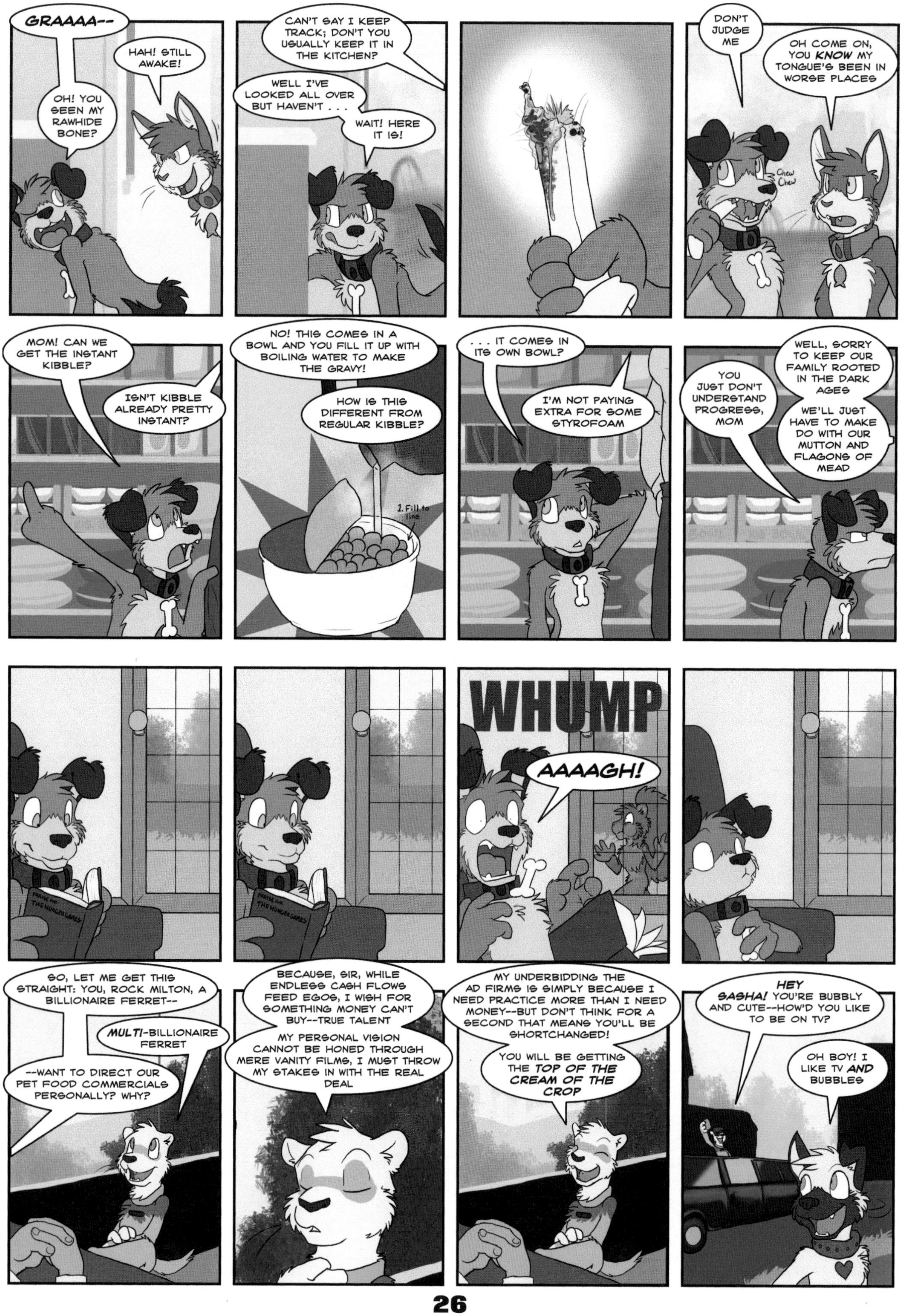
GRAAAA--
HAH! STILL AWAKE!
OH! YOU SEEN MY RAWHIDE BONE?
CAN'T SAY I KEEP TRACK; DON'T YOU USUALLY KEEP IT IN THE KITCHEN?
WELL I'VE LOOKED ALL OVER BUT HAVEN'T . . .
WAIT! HERE IT IS!
DON'T JUDGE ME
OH COME ON, YOU KNOW MY TONGUE'S BEEN IN WORSE PLACES
Chew Chew
MOM! CAN WE GET THE INSTANT KIBBLE?
ISN'T KIBBLE ALREADY PRETTY INSTANT?
NO! THIS COMES IN A BOWL AND YOU FILL IT UP WITH BOILING WATER TO MAKE THE GRAVY!
HOW IS THIS DIFFERENT FROM REGULAR KIBBLE?
1. Fill to line
. . . IT COMES IN ITS OWN BOWL?
I'M NOT PAYING EXTRA FOR SOME STYROFOAM
YOU JUST DON'T UNDERSTAND PROGRESS, MOM
WELL, SORRY TO KEEP OUR FAMILY ROOTED IN THE DARK AGES
WE'LL JUST HAVE TO MAKE DO WITH OUR MUTTON AND FLAGONS OF MEAD
THE HUNGER GAMES
THE HUNGER GAMES
WHUMP
AAAAGH!
SO, LET ME GET THIS STRAIGHT: YOU, ROCK MILTON, A BILLIONAIRE FERRET--
MULTI-BILLIONAIRE FERRET
--WANT TO DIRECT OUR PET FOOD COMMERCIALS PERSONALLY? WHY?
BECAUSE, SIR, WHILE ENDLESS CASH FLOWS FEED EGOS, I WISH FOR SOMETHING MONEY CAN'T BUY--TRUE TALENT
MY PERSONAL VISION CANNOT BE HONED THROUGH MERE VANITY FILMS, I MUST THROW MY STAKES IN WITH THE REAL DEAL
MY UNDERBIDDING THE AD FIRMS IS SIMPLY BECAUSE I NEED PRACTICE MORE THAN I NEED MONEY--BUT DON'T THINK FOR A SECOND THAT MEANS YOU'LL BE SHORTCHANGED!
YOU WILL BE GETTING THE TOP OF THE CREAM OF THE CROP
HEY SASHA! YOU'RE BUBBLY AND CUTE--HOW'D YOU LIKE TO BE ON TV?
OH BOY! I LIKE TV AND BUBBLES

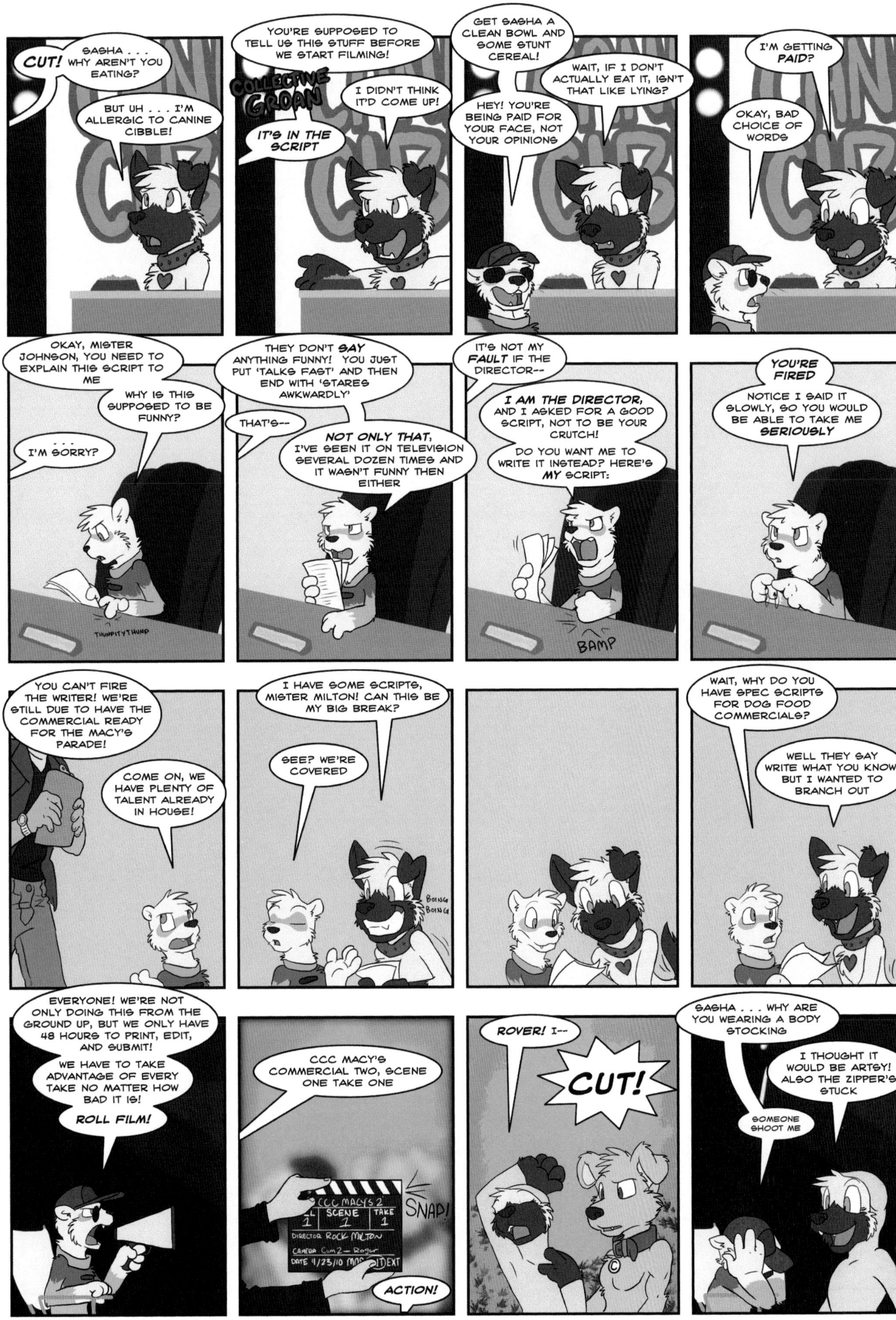
CUT!
SASHA . . . WHY AREN'T YOU EATING?
BUT UH . . . I'M ALLERGIC TO CANINE CIBBLE!
YOU'RE SUPPOSED TO TELL US THIS STUFF BEFORE WE START FILMING!
COLLECTIVE GROAN
I DIDN'T THINK IT'D COME UP!
IT'S IN THE SCRIPT
GET SASHA A CLEAN BOWL AND SOME STUNT CEREAL!
WAIT, IF I DON'T ACTUALLY EAT IT, ISN'T THAT LIKE LYING?
HEY! YOU'RE BEING PAID FOR YOUR FACE, NOT YOUR OPINIONS
I'M GETTING PAID?
OKAY, BAD CHOICE OF WORDS
OKAY, MISTER JOHNSON, YOU NEED TO EXPLAIN THIS SCRIPT TO ME
WHY IS THIS SUPPOSED TO BE FUNNY?
. . . I'M SORRY?
THUMPITYTHUMP
THEY DON'T SAY ANYTHING FUNNY! YOU JUST PUT 'TALKS FAST' AND THEN END WITH 'STARES AWKWARDLY'
THAT'S--
NOT ONLY THAT, I'VE SEEN IT ON TELEVISION SEVERAL DOZEN TIMES AND IT WASN'T FUNNY THEN EITHER
IT'S NOT MY FAULT IF THE DIRECTOR--
I AM THE DIRECTOR, AND I ASKED FOR A GOOD SCRIPT, NOT TO BE YOUR CRUTCH!
DO YOU WANT ME TO WRITE IT INSTEAD? HERE'S MY SCRIPT:
BAMP
YOU'RE FIRED
NOTICE I SAID IT SLOWLY, SO YOU WOULD BE ABLE TO TAKE ME SERIOUSLY
YOU CAN'T FIRE THE WRITER! WE'RE STILL DUE TO HAVE THE COMMERCIAL READY FOR THE MACY'S PARADE!
COME ON, WE HAVE PLENTY OF TALENT ALREADY IN HOUSE!
I HAVE SOME SCRIPTS, MISTER MILTON! CAN THIS BE MY BIG BREAK?
SEE? WE'RE COVERED
BOING BOING
WAIT, WHY DO YOU HAVE SPEC SCRIPTS FOR DOG FOOD COMMERCIALS?
WELL THEY SAY WRITE WHAT YOU KNOW, BUT I WANTED TO BRANCH OUT
EVERYONE! WE'RE NOT ONLY DOING THIS FROM THE GROUND UP, BUT WE ONLY HAVE 48 HOURS TO PRINT, EDIT, AND SUBMIT!
WE HAVE TO TAKE ADVANTAGE OF EVERY TAKE NO MATTER HOW BAD IT IS!
ROLL FILM!
CCC MACY'S COMMERCIAL TWO, SCENE ONE TAKE ONE
CCC MACYS 2
SCENE 1 TAKE 1
DIRECTOR ROCK MILTON
SNAP!
ACTION!
ROVER! I--
CUT!
SASHA . . . WHY ARE YOU WEARING A BODY STOCKING
I THOUGHT IT WOULD BE ARTSY! ALSO THE ZIPPER'S STUCK
SOMEONE SHOOT ME

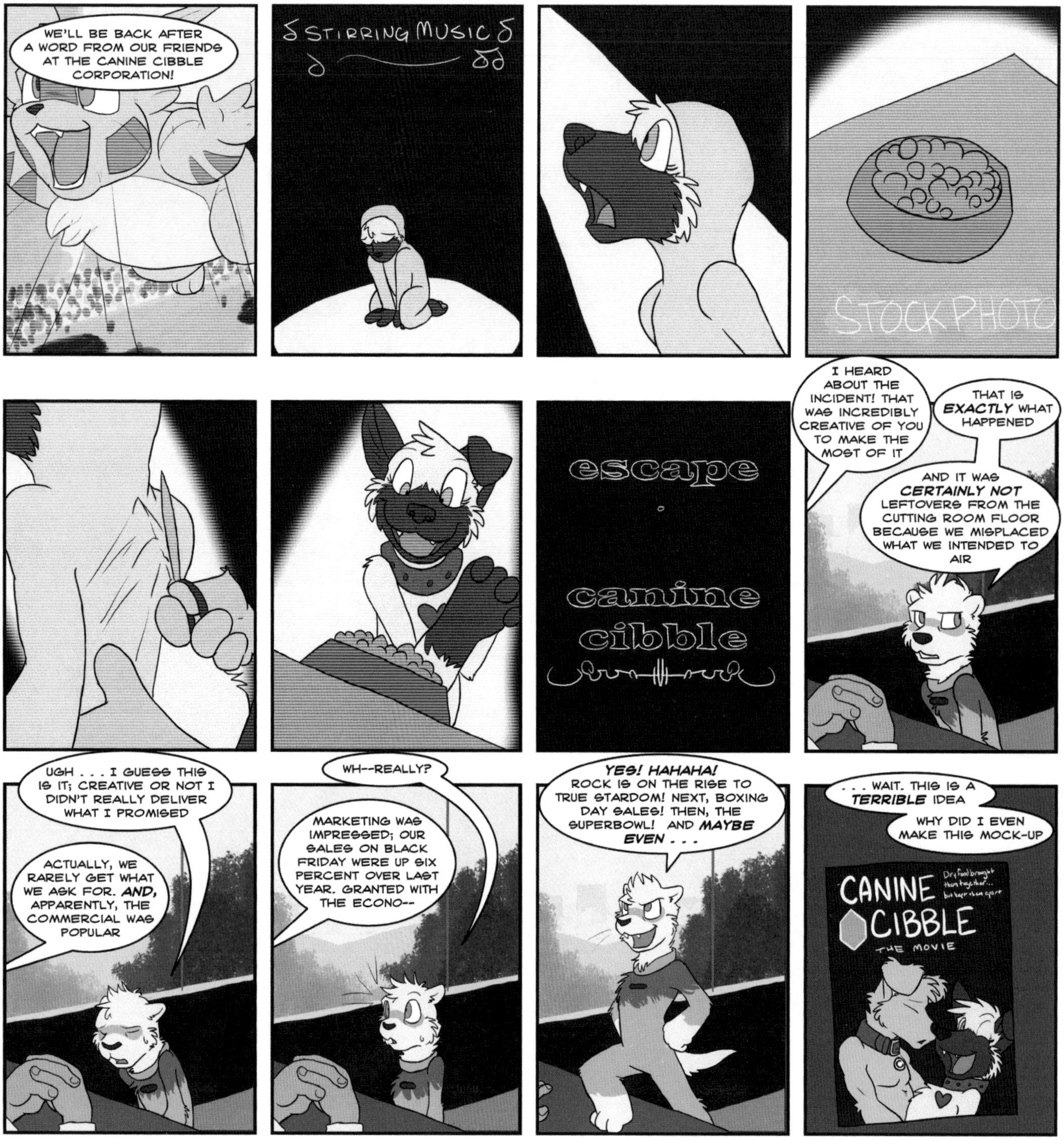
WE'LL BE BACK AFTER A WORD FROM OUR FRIENDS AT THE CANINE CIBBLE CORPORATION!
STIRRING MUSIC
STOCK PHOTO
escape
canine cibble
I HEARD ABOUT THE INCIDENT! THAT WAS INCREDIBLY CREATIVE OF YOU TO MAKE THE MOST OF IT
THAT IS *EXACTLY* WHAT HAPPENED
AND IT WAS *CERTAINLY NOT* LEFTOVERS FROM THE CUTTING ROOM FLOOR BECAUSE WE MISPLACED WHAT WE INTENDED TO AIR
UGH . . . I GUESS THIS IS IT; CREATIVE OR NOT I DIDN'T REALLY DELIVER WHAT I PROMISED
ACTUALLY, WE RARELY GET WHAT WE ASK FOR. ***AND,*** APPARENTLY, THE COMMERCIAL WAS POPULAR
WH--REALLY?
MARKETING WAS IMPRESSED; OUR SALES ON BLACK FRIDAY WERE UP SIX PERCENT OVER LAST YEAR. GRANTED WITH THE ECONO--
YES! HAHAHA! ROCK IS ON THE RISE TO TRUE STARDOM! NEXT, BOXING DAY SALES! THEN, THE SUPERBOWL! AND ***MAYBE EVEN*** . . .
. . . WAIT. THIS IS A ***TERRIBLE*** IDEA
WHY DID I EVEN MAKE THIS MOCK-UP
CANINE CIBBLE
THE MOVIE

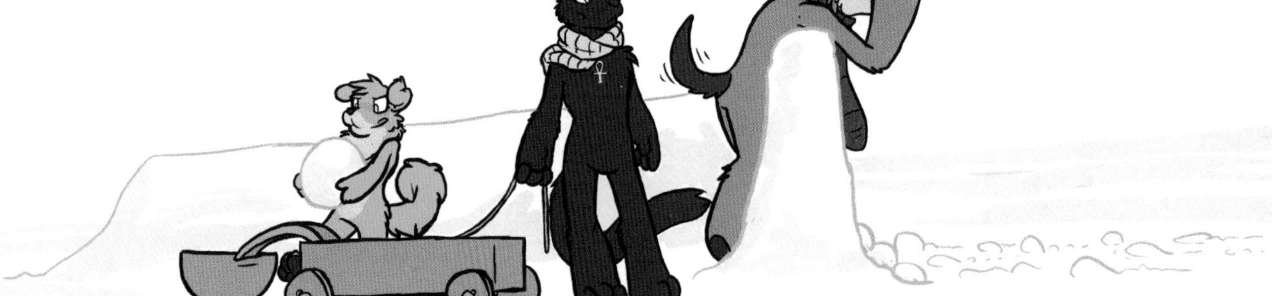

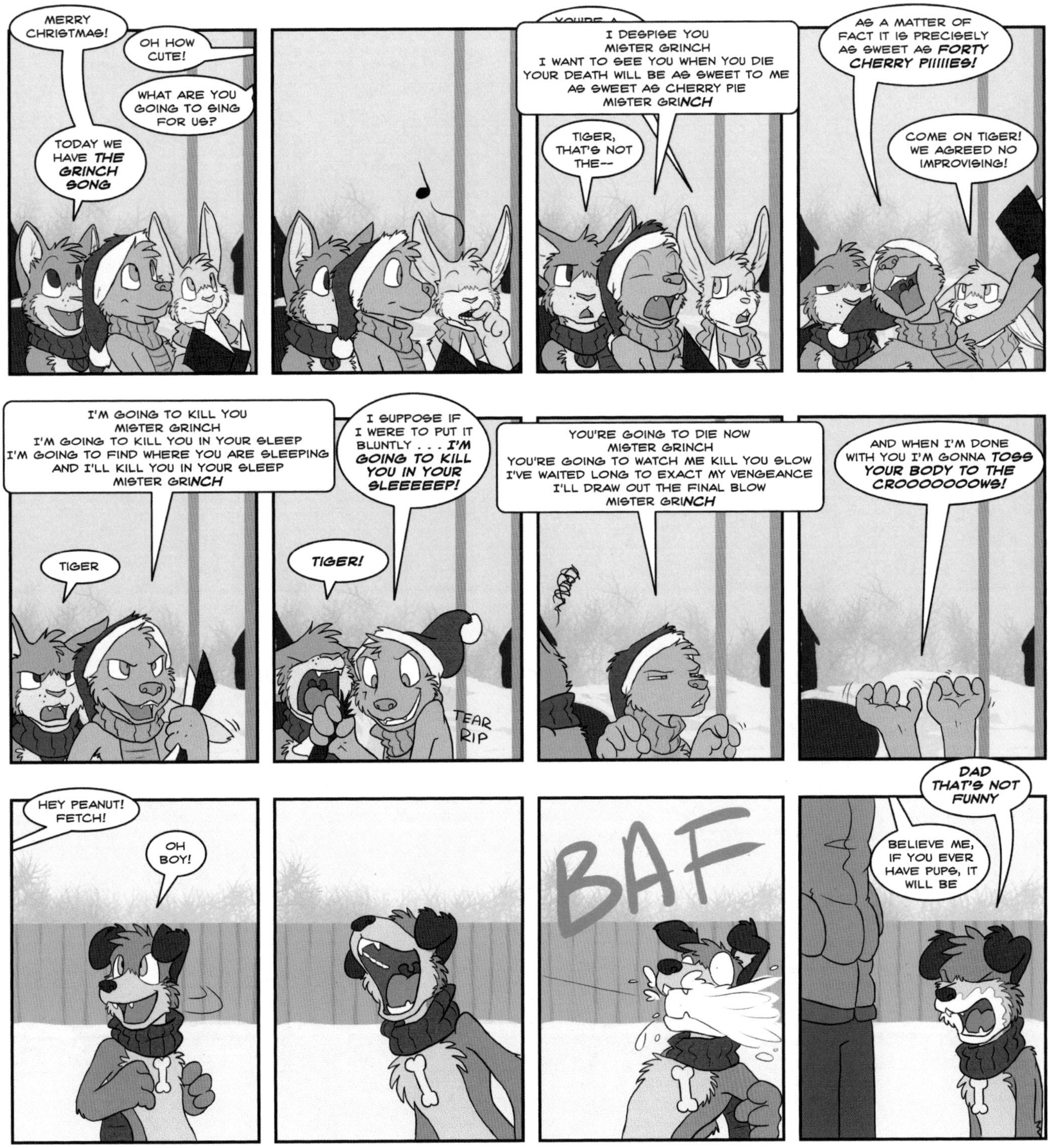
MERRY CHRISTMAS!
OH HOW CUTE!
WHAT ARE YOU GOING TO SING FOR US?
TODAY WE HAVE THE GRINCH SONG
I DESPISE YOU
MISTER GRINCH
I WANT TO SEE YOU WHEN YOU DIE
YOUR DEATH WILL BE AS SWEET TO ME
AS SWEET AS CHERRY PIE
MISTER GRINCH
TIGER, THAT'S NOT THE--
AS A MATTER OF FACT IT IS PRECISELY AS SWEET AS FORTY CHERRY PIIIIIES!
COME ON TIGER! WE AGREED NO IMPROVISING!
I'M GOING TO KILL YOU
MISTER GRINCH
I'M GOING TO KILL YOU IN YOUR SLEEP
I'M GOING TO FIND WHERE YOU ARE SLEEPING
AND I'LL KILL YOU IN YOUR SLEEP
MISTER GRINCH
TIGER
I SUPPOSE IF I WERE TO PUT IT BLUNTLY . . . I'M GOING TO KILL YOU IN YOUR SLEEEEEP!
TIGER!
TEAR RIP
YOU'RE GOING TO DIE NOW
MISTER GRINCH
YOU'RE GOING TO WATCH ME KILL YOU SLOW
I'VE WAITED LONG TO EXACT MY VENGEANCE
I'LL DRAW OUT THE FINAL BLOW
MISTER GRINCH
AND WHEN I'M DONE WITH YOU I'M GONNA TOSS YOUR BODY TO THE CROOOOOOOWS!
HEY PEANUT! FETCH!
OH BOY!
BAF
DAD THAT'S NOT FUNNY
BELIEVE ME, IF YOU EVER HAVE PUPS, IT WILL BE

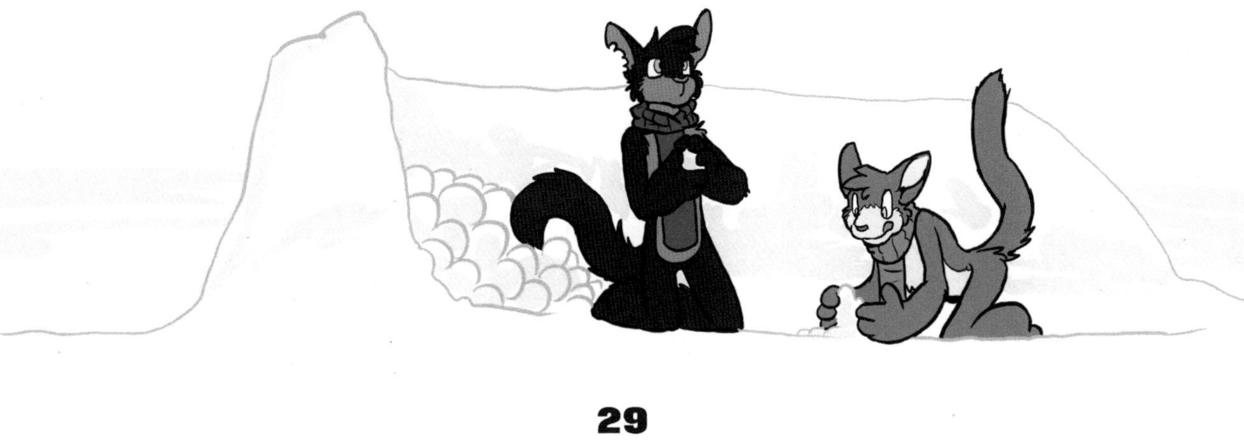

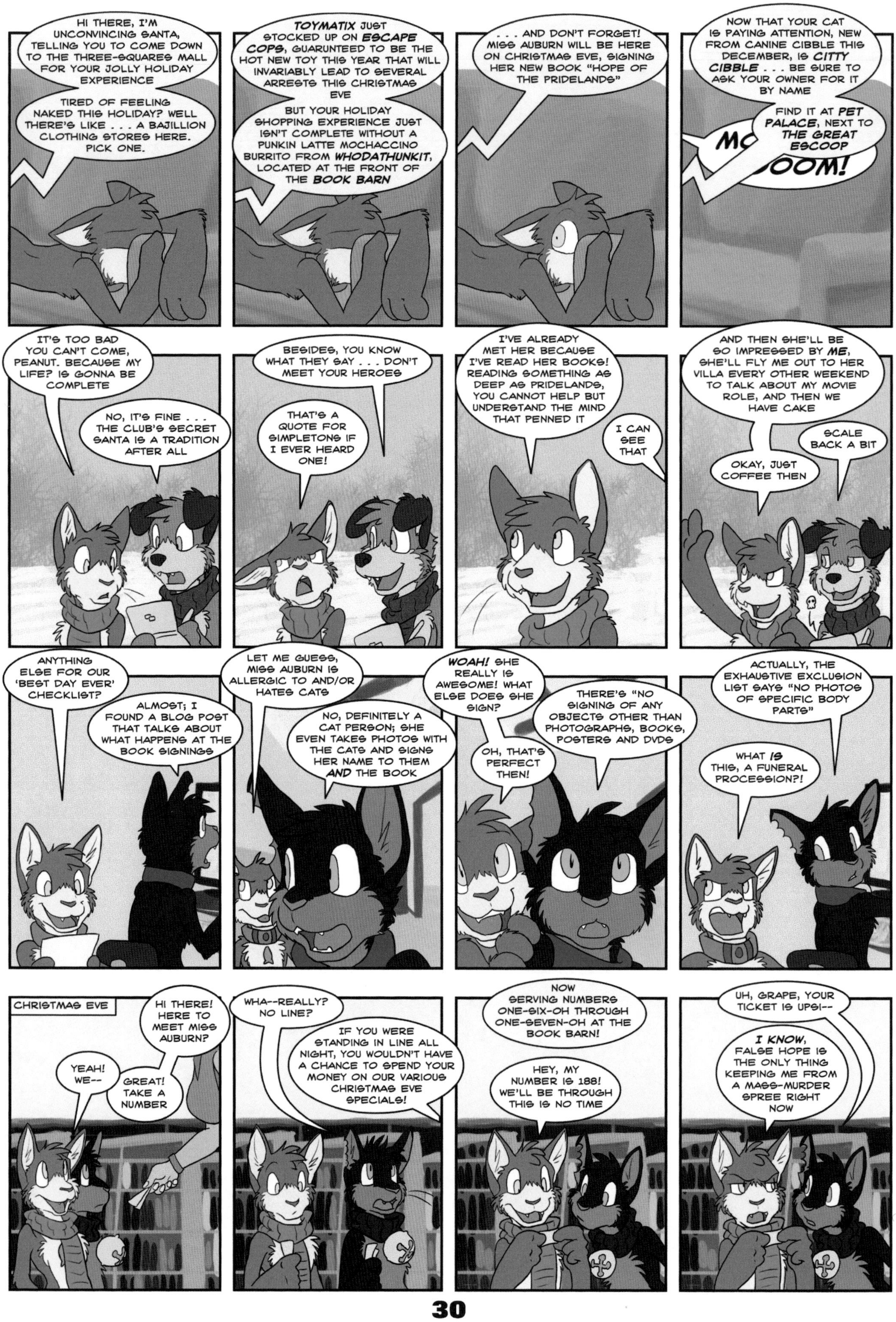
HI THERE, I'M UNCONVINCING SANTA, TELLING YOU TO COME DOWN TO THE THREE-SQUARES MALL FOR YOUR JOLLY HOLIDAY EXPERIENCE
TIRED OF FEELING NAKED THIS HOLIDAY? WELL THERE'S LIKE . . . A BAJILLION CLOTHING STORES HERE. PICK ONE.
TOYMATIX JUST STOCKED UP ON ESCAPE COPS, GUARUNTEED TO BE THE HOT NEW TOY THIS YEAR THAT WILL INVARIABLY LEAD TO SEVERAL ARRESTS THIS CHRISTMAS EVE
BUT YOUR HOLIDAY SHOPPING EXPERIENCE JUST ISN'T COMPLETE WITHOUT A PUNKIN LATTE MOCHACCINO BURRITO FROM WHODATHUNKIT, LOCATED AT THE FRONT OF THE BOOK BARN
. . . AND DON'T FORGET! MISS AUBURN WILL BE HERE ON CHRISTMAS EVE, SIGNING HER NEW BOOK "HOPE OF THE PRIDELANDS"
NOW THAT YOUR CAT IS PAYING ATTENTION, NEW FROM CANINE CIBBLE THIS DECEMBER, IS CITTY CIBBLE . . . BE SURE TO ASK YOUR OWNER FOR IT BY NAME
FIND IT AT PET PALACE, NEXT TO THE GREAT ESCOOP
MO
OOM!
IT'S TOO BAD YOU CAN'T COME, PEANUT. BECAUSE MY LIFE? IS GONNA BE COMPLETE
NO, IT'S FINE . . . THE CLUB'S SECRET SANTA IS A TRADITION AFTER ALL
BESIDES, YOU KNOW WHAT THEY SAY . . . DON'T MEET YOUR HEROES
THAT'S A QUOTE FOR SIMPLETONS IF I EVER HEARD ONE!
I'VE ALREADY MET HER BECAUSE I'VE READ HER BOOKS! READING SOMETHING AS DEEP AS PRIDELANDS, YOU CANNOT HELP BUT UNDERSTAND THE MIND THAT PENNED IT
I CAN SEE THAT
AND THEN SHE'LL BE SO IMPRESSED BY ME, SHE'LL FLY ME OUT TO HER VILLA EVERY OTHER WEEKEND TO TALK ABOUT MY MOVIE ROLE, AND THEN WE HAVE CAKE
SCALE BACK A BIT
OKAY, JUST COFFEE THEN
ANYTHING ELSE FOR OUR 'BEST DAY EVER' CHECKLIST?
ALMOST; I FOUND A BLOG POST THAT TALKS ABOUT WHAT HAPPENS AT THE BOOK SIGNINGS
LET ME GUESS, MISS AUBURN IS ALLERGIC TO AND/OR HATES CATS
NO, DEFINITELY A CAT PERSON; SHE EVEN TAKES PHOTOS WITH THE CATS AND SIGNS HER NAME TO THEM AND THE BOOK
WOAH! SHE REALLY IS AWESOME! WHAT ELSE DOES SHE SIGN?
THERE'S "NO SIGNING OF ANY OBJECTS OTHER THAN PHOTOGRAPHS, BOOKS, POSTERS AND DVDS
OH, THAT'S PERFECT THEN!
ACTUALLY, THE EXHAUSTIVE EXCLUSION LIST SAYS "NO PHOTOS OF SPECIFIC BODY PARTS"
WHAT IS THIS, A FUNERAL PROCESSION?!
CHRISTMAS EVE
HI THERE! HERE TO MEET MISS AUBURN?
YEAH! WE--
GREAT! TAKE A NUMBER
WHA--REALLY? NO LINE?
IF YOU WERE STANDING IN LINE ALL NIGHT, YOU WOULDN'T HAVE A CHANCE TO SPEND YOUR MONEY ON OUR VARIOUS CHRISTMAS EVE SPECIALS!
NOW SERVING NUMBERS ONE-SIX-OH THROUGH ONE-SEVEN-OH AT THE BOOK BARN!
HEY, MY NUMBER IS 188! WE'LL BE THROUGH THIS IS NO TIME
UH, GRAPE, YOUR TICKET IS UPSI--
I KNOW, FALSE HOPE IS THE ONLY THING KEEPING ME FROM A MASS-MURDER SPREE RIGHT NOW

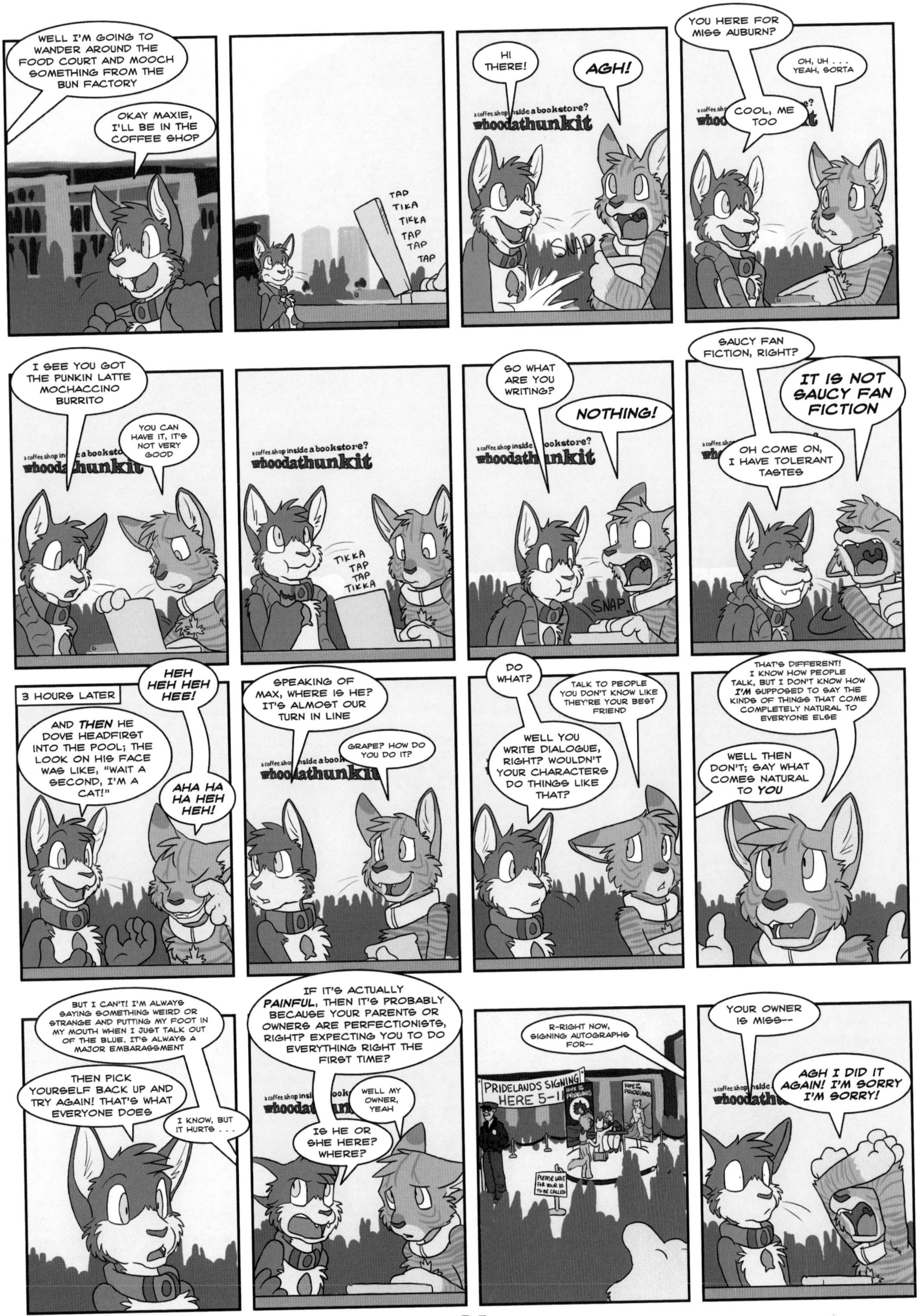
WELL I'M GOING TO WANDER AROUND THE FOOD COURT AND MOOCH SOMETHING FROM THE BUN FACTORY
OKAY MAXIE, I'LL BE IN THE COFFEE SHOP
TAP TIKA TIKKA TAP TAP TAP
a coffee shop inside a bookstore? whoodathunkit
HI THERE!
AGH!
SNAP
YOU HERE FOR MISS AUBURN?
OH, UH . . . YEAH, SORTA
COOL, ME TOO
I SEE YOU GOT THE PUNKIN LATTE MOCHACCINO BURRITO
YOU CAN HAVE IT, IT'S NOT VERY GOOD
TIKKA TAP TAP TIKKA
SO WHAT ARE YOU WRITING?
NOTHING!
SNAP
SAUCY FAN FICTION, RIGHT?
IT IS NOT SAUCY FAN FICTION
OH COME ON, I HAVE TOLERANT TASTES
3 HOURS LATER
HEH HEH HEH HEE!
AND THEN HE DOVE HEADFIRST INTO THE POOL; THE LOOK ON HIS FACE WAS LIKE, "WAIT A SECOND, I'M A CAT!"
AHA HA HA HEH HEH!
SPEAKING OF MAX, WHERE IS HE? IT'S ALMOST OUR TURN IN LINE
GRAPE? HOW DO YOU DO IT?
DO WHAT?
TALK TO PEOPLE YOU DON'T KNOW LIKE THEY'RE YOUR BEST FRIEND
WELL YOU WRITE DIALOGUE, RIGHT? WOULDN'T YOUR CHARACTERS DO THINGS LIKE THAT?
THAT'S DIFFERENT! I KNOW HOW PEOPLE TALK, BUT I DON'T KNOW HOW I'M SUPPOSED TO SAY THE KINDS OF THINGS THAT COME COMPLETELY NATURAL TO EVERYONE ELSE
WELL THEN DON'T; SAY WHAT COMES NATURAL TO YOU
BUT I CAN'T! I'M ALWAYS SAYING SOMETHING WEIRD OR STRANGE AND PUTTING MY FOOT IN MY MOUTH WHEN I JUST TALK OUT OF THE BLUE. IT'S ALWAYS A MAJOR EMBARASSMENT
THEN PICK YOURSELF BACK UP AND TRY AGAIN! THAT'S WHAT EVERYONE DOES
I KNOW, BUT IT HURTS . . .
IF IT'S ACTUALLY PAINFUL, THEN IT'S PROBABLY BECAUSE YOUR PARENTS OR OWNERS ARE PERFECTIONISTS, RIGHT? EXPECTING YOU TO DO EVERYTHING RIGHT THE FIRST TIME?
WELL MY OWNER, YEAH
IS HE OR SHE HERE? WHERE?
R-RIGHT NOW, SIGNING AUTOGRAPHS FOR--
PRIDELANDS SIGNING HERE 5-11
YOUR OWNER IS MISS--
AGH I DID IT AGAIN! I'M SORRY I'M SORRY!

RES . . . I'M GETTING A DREAD FEELING WITH YOU LOOKING LIKE THAT
PLEASE TELL ME THE CAT-ORIENTED BOOK FOR CATS THAT PRECISELY DETAILS CAT EXPERIENCES WAS NOT WRITTEN BY A CAT
. . . SORRY
. . . RES, IS YOUR OWNER TAKING ALL THE CREDIT FOR YOUR STORY?
WELL SHE HELPS, SHE DOES THE EDITING FOR US AND . . .
OKAY THAT'S IT, I AM GOING TO GO OVER THERE AND GIVE HER A PIECE OF MY IRRATIONAL ANGER
GRAPE, YOU DON'T UNDERSTAND, I ASKED HER TO **WAIT COME BACK**
IN ALL HONESTY MRS. SANDWICH, I THOUGHT PHYSICALLY ***CHUCKING*** SOMEONE OFF THE PREMISES WAS ONLY SOMETHING ***YOU*** DID
MAX, HUSH
GRAPE, IF YOU DON'T MIND ME ASKING, AND I KNOW YOU DON'T . . . ***WHAT IN SANTA'S NAME WERE YOU THINKING?!***
I DON'T KNOW!
I PANICKED, OKAY? WATCHING RES'S BEHAVIOR I WAS SURE THERE WAS SOMETHING WRONG GOING ON . . . AND IT DIDN'T MATTER IF RES OBJECTED BECAUSE THAT JUST MEANT HE WAS BEING BULLIED INTO THINKING IT WAS OKAY, RIGHT?
DID YOU KNOW THERE WAS A WOLF ACTOR IN THE 30'S WHO HAD HIS TAIL CUT OFF SO HE COULD PLAY A WEREWOLF? IT'S SICK, RIGHT? IT STILL GOES ON, EVERYONE KNOWS IT DOES . . . AND I WAS SURE IT WAS ONE OF THOSE TIMES . . .
BUT LOOKING AT HIM AS I WENT OUT, I WONDERED, IF THAT WAS THE CASE, WHAT WAS HE DOING IN PUBLIC? WHY WAS I ABLE TO TALK TO HIM?
AND NOW I'M SCARED
I . . . I THINK I RUINED MY CHANCES AT HAVING THE BEST FRIEND EVER
THAT'S NOT COUNTING ME, RIGHT?
SO HELP ME MAX I WILL SUCK DOWN A CANDY CANE TIP AND STAB YOU WITH IT

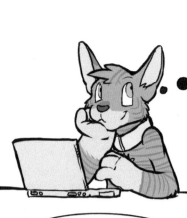

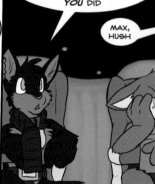

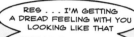

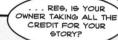

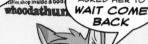

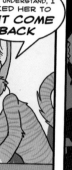

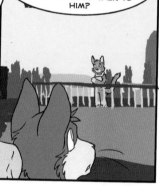

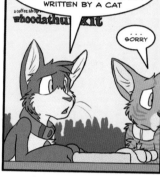

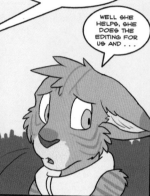

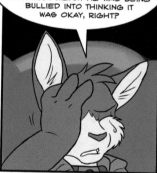

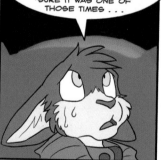

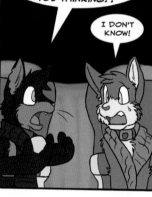

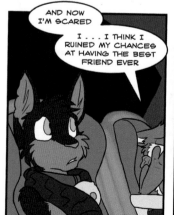

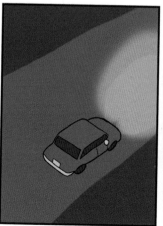

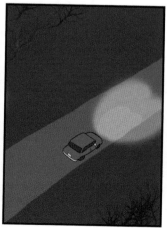

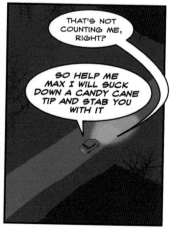

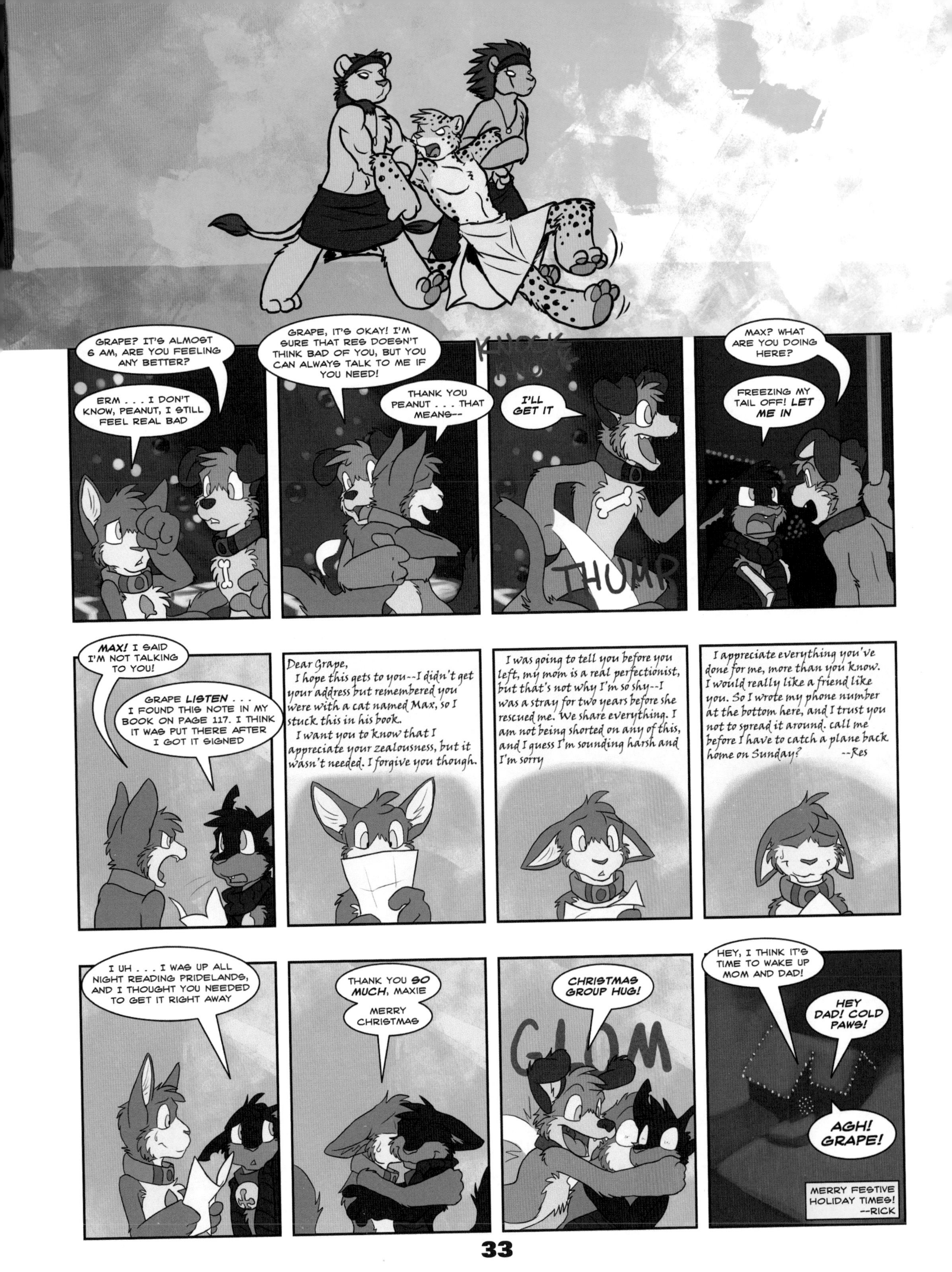
GRAPE? IT'S ALMOST 6 AM, ARE YOU FEELING ANY BETTER?
ERM . . . I DON'T KNOW, PEANUT, I STILL FEEL REAL BAD
GRAPE, IT'S OKAY! I'M SURE THAT RES DOESN'T THINK BAD OF YOU, BUT YOU CAN ALWAYS TALK TO ME IF YOU NEED!
THANK YOU PEANUT . . . THAT MEANS--
KNOCK KNOCK
I'LL GET IT
THUMP
MAX? WHAT ARE YOU DOING HERE?
FREEZING MY TAIL OFF! LET ME IN
MAX! I SAID I'M NOT TALKING TO YOU!
GRAPE LISTEN . . . I FOUND THIS NOTE IN MY BOOK ON PAGE 117. I THINK IT WAS PUT THERE AFTER I GOT IT SIGNED
Dear Grape,
I hope this gets to you--I didn't get your address but remembered you were with a cat named Max, so I stuck this in his book.
I want you to know that I appreciate your zealousness, but it wasn't needed. I forgive you though.
I was going to tell you before you left, my mom is a real perfectionist, but that's not why I'm so shy--I was a stray for two years before she rescued me. We share everything. I am not being shorted on any of this, and I guess I'm sounding harsh and I'm sorry
I appreciate everything you've done for me, more than you know. I would really like a friend like you. So I wrote my phone number at the bottom here, and I trust you not to spread it around. call me before I have to catch a plane back home on Sunday? --Res
I UH . . . I WAS UP ALL NIGHT READING PRIDELANDS, AND I THOUGHT YOU NEEDED TO GET IT RIGHT AWAY
THANK YOU SO MUCH, MAXIE
MERRY CHRISTMAS
CHRISTMAS GROUP HUG!
GLOM
HEY, I THINK IT'S TIME TO WAKE UP MOM AND DAD!
HEY DAD! COLD PAWS!
AGH! GRAPE!
MERRY FESTIVE HOLIDAY TIMES! --RICK

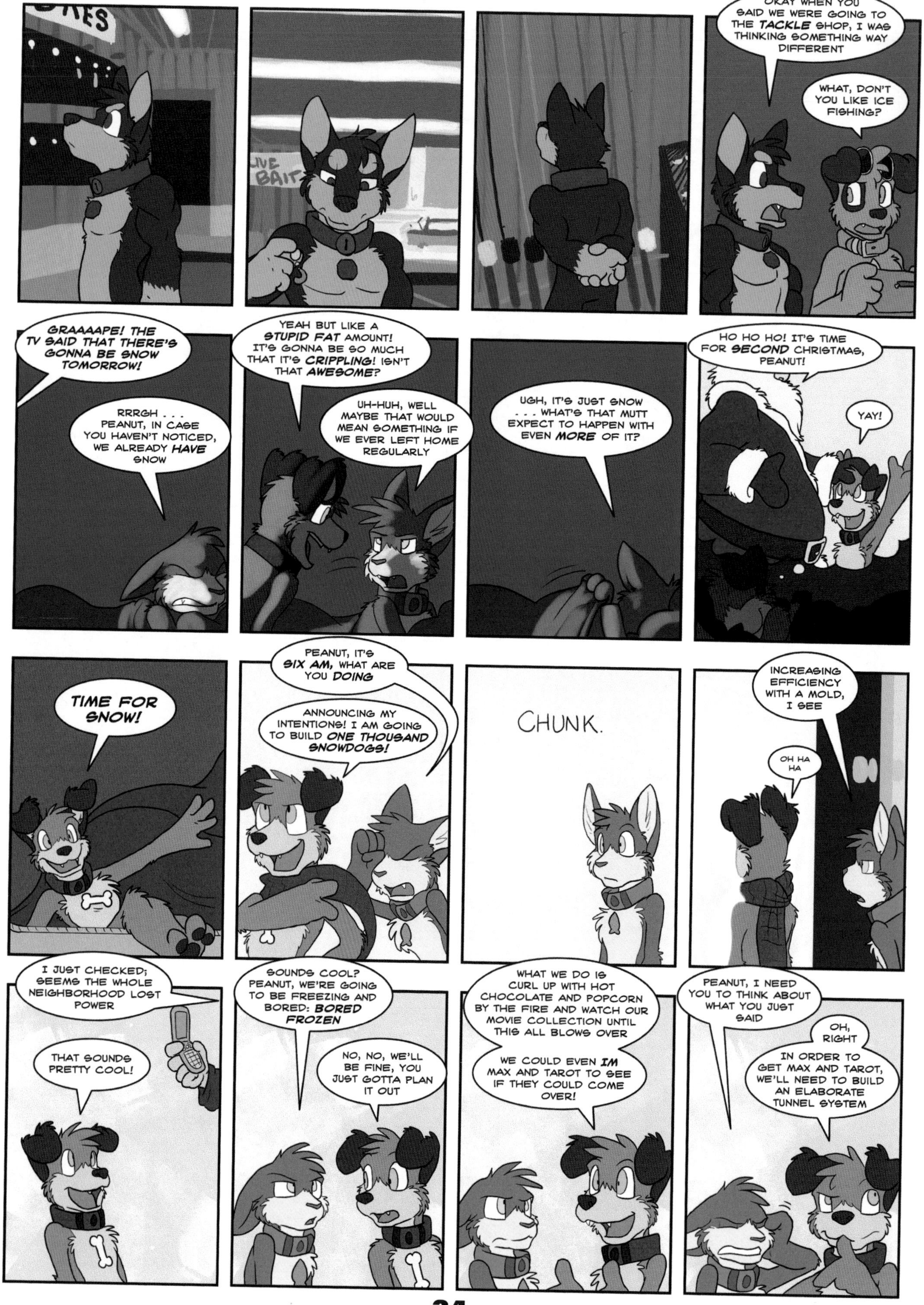
LIVE BAIT
OKAY WHEN YOU SAID WE WERE GOING TO THE TACKLE SHOP, I WAS THINKING SOMETHING WAY DIFFERENT
WHAT, DON'T YOU LIKE ICE FISHING?
GRAAAAPE! THE TV SAID THAT THERE'S GONNA BE SNOW TOMORROW!
RRRGH . . . PEANUT, IN CASE YOU HAVEN'T NOTICED, WE ALREADY HAVE SNOW
YEAH BUT LIKE A STUPID FAT AMOUNT! IT'S GONNA BE SO MUCH THAT IT'S CRIPPLING! ISN'T THAT AWESOME?
UH-HUH, WELL MAYBE THAT WOULD MEAN SOMETHING IF WE EVER LEFT HOME REGULARLY
UGH, IT'S JUST SNOW . . . WHAT'S THAT MUTT EXPECT TO HAPPEN WITH EVEN MORE OF IT?
HO HO HO! IT'S TIME FOR SECOND CHRISTMAS, PEANUT!
YAY!
TIME FOR SNOW!
PEANUT, IT'S SIX AM, WHAT ARE YOU DOING
ANNOUNCING MY INTENTIONS! I AM GOING TO BUILD ONE THOUSAND SNOWDOGS!
CHUNK.
INCREASING EFFICIENCY WITH A MOLD, I SEE
OH HA HA
I JUST CHECKED; SEEMS THE WHOLE NEIGHBORHOOD LOST POWER
THAT SOUNDS PRETTY COOL!
SOUNDS COOL? PEANUT, WE'RE GOING TO BE FREEZING AND BORED: BORED FROZEN
NO, NO, WE'LL BE FINE, YOU JUST GOTTA PLAN IT OUT
WHAT WE DO IS CURL UP WITH HOT CHOCOLATE AND POPCORN BY THE FIRE AND WATCH OUR MOVIE COLLECTION UNTIL THIS ALL BLOWS OVER
WE COULD EVEN IM MAX AND TAROT TO SEE IF THEY COULD COME OVER!
PEANUT, I NEED YOU TO THINK ABOUT WHAT YOU JUST SAID
OH, RIGHT
IN ORDER TO GET MAX AND TAROT, WE'LL NEED TO BUILD AN ELABORATE TUNNEL SYSTEM

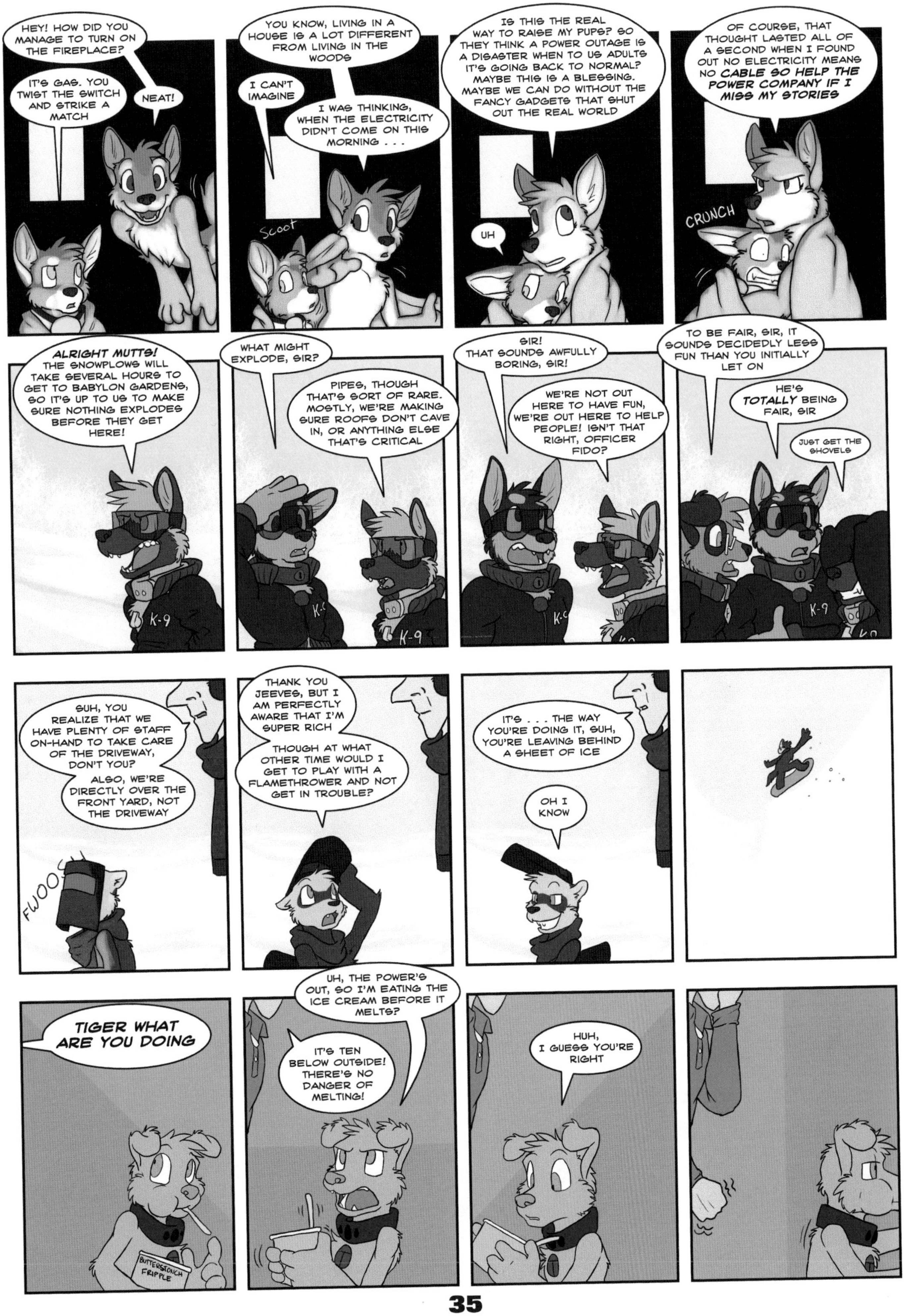
HEY! HOW DID YOU MANAGE TO TURN ON THE FIREPLACE?
IT'S GAS. YOU TWIST THE SWITCH AND STRIKE A MATCH
NEAT!
YOU KNOW, LIVING IN A HOUSE IS A LOT DIFFERENT FROM LIVING IN THE WOODS
I CAN'T IMAGINE
I WAS THINKING, WHEN THE ELECTRICITY DIDN'T COME ON THIS MORNING . . .
SCOOT
IS THIS THE REAL WAY TO RAISE MY PUPS? SO THEY THINK A POWER OUTAGE IS A DISASTER WHEN TO US ADULTS IT'S GOING BACK TO NORMAL? MAYBE THIS IS A BLESSING. MAYBE WE CAN DO WITHOUT THE FANCY GADGETS THAT SHUT OUT THE REAL WORLD
UH
OF COURSE, THAT THOUGHT LASTED ALL OF A SECOND WHEN I FOUND OUT NO ELECTRICITY MEANS NO CABLE SO HELP THE POWER COMPANY IF I MISS MY STORIES
CRUNCH
ALRIGHT MUTTS! THE SNOWPLOWS WILL TAKE SEVERAL HOURS TO GET TO BABYLON GARDENS, SO IT'S UP TO US TO MAKE SURE NOTHING EXPLODES BEFORE THEY GET HERE!
K-9
WHAT MIGHT EXPLODE, SIR?
PIPES, THOUGH THAT'S SORT OF RARE. MOSTLY, WE'RE MAKING SURE ROOFS DON'T CAVE IN, OR ANYTHING ELSE THAT'S CRITICAL
K-9
SIR! THAT SOUNDS AWFULLY BORING, SIR!
WE'RE NOT OUT HERE TO HAVE FUN, WE'RE OUT HERE TO HELP PEOPLE! ISN'T THAT RIGHT, OFFICER FIDO?
TO BE FAIR, SIR, IT SOUNDS DECIDEDLY LESS FUN THAN YOU INITIALLY LET ON
HE'S TOTALLY BEING FAIR, SIR
JUST GET THE SHOVELS
K-9
SUH, YOU REALIZE THAT WE HAVE PLENTY OF STAFF ON-HAND TO TAKE CARE OF THE DRIVEWAY, DON'T YOU?
ALSO, WE'RE DIRECTLY OVER THE FRONT YARD, NOT THE DRIVEWAY
FWOO
THANK YOU JEEVES, BUT I AM PERFECTLY AWARE THAT I'M SUPER RICH
THOUGH AT WHAT OTHER TIME WOULD I GET TO PLAY WITH A FLAMETHROWER AND NOT GET IN TROUBLE?
IT'S . . . THE WAY YOU'RE DOING IT, SUH, YOU'RE LEAVING BEHIND A SHEET OF ICE
OH I KNOW
TIGER WHAT ARE YOU DOING
BUTTERSCOTCH FRIPPLE
UH, THE POWER'S OUT, SO I'M EATING THE ICE CREAM BEFORE IT MELTS?
IT'S TEN BELOW OUTSIDE! THERE'S NO DANGER OF MELTING!
HUH, I GUESS YOU'RE RIGHT

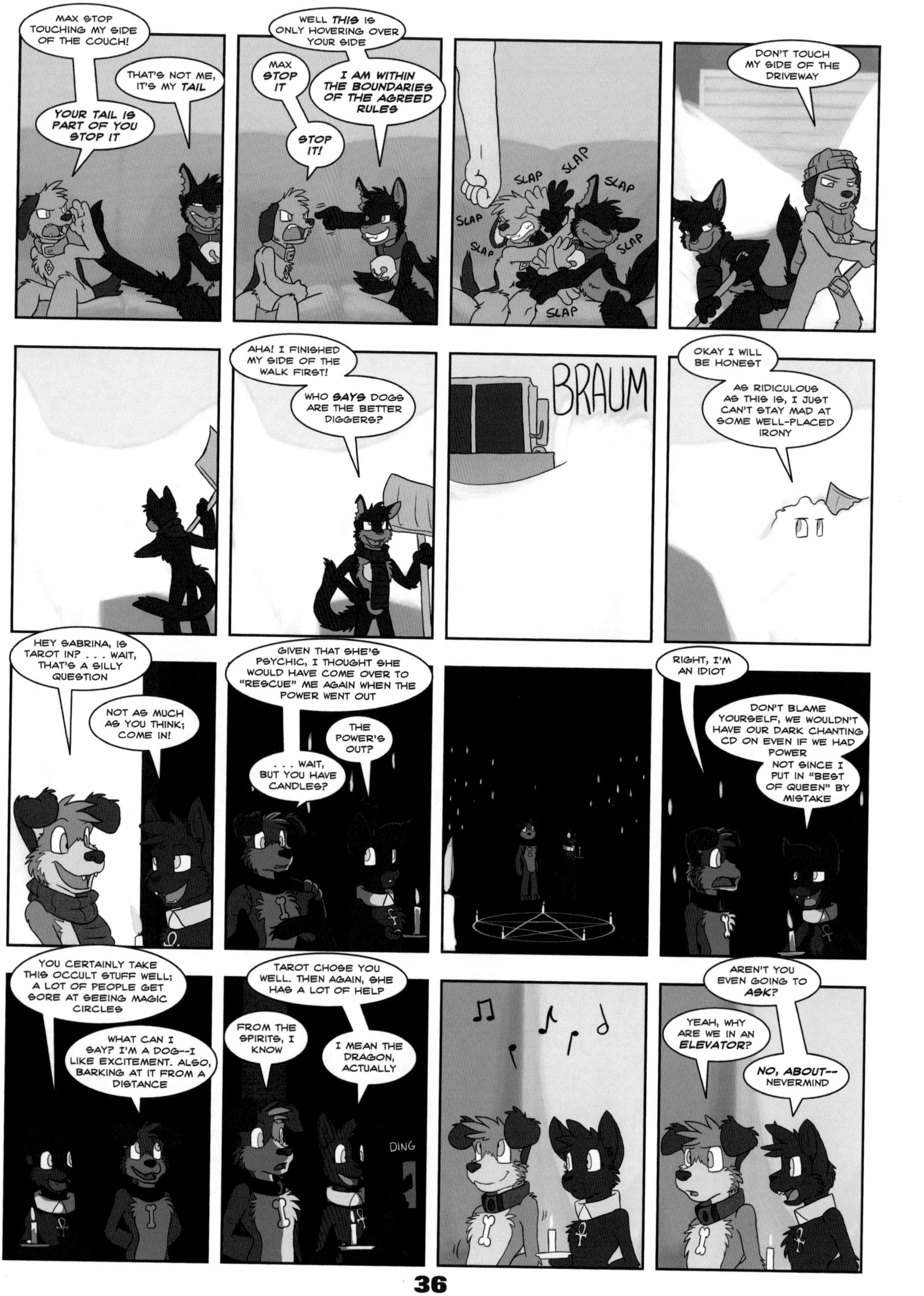
MAX STOP TOUCHING MY SIDE OF THE COUCH!
THAT'S NOT ME, IT'S MY TAIL
YOUR TAIL IS PART OF YOU STOP IT
WELL THIS IS ONLY HOVERING OVER YOUR SIDE
MAX STOP IT
I AM WITHIN THE BOUNDARIES OF THE AGREED RULES
STOP IT!
SLAP SLAP SLAP SLAP SLAP SLAP SLAP
DON'T TOUCH MY SIDE OF THE DRIVEWAY
AHA! I FINISHED MY SIDE OF THE WALK FIRST!
WHO SAYS DOGS ARE THE BETTER DIGGERS?
BRAUM
OKAY I WILL BE HONEST
AS RIDICULOUS AS THIS IS, I JUST CAN'T STAY MAD AT SOME WELL-PLACED IRONY
HEY SABRINA, IS TAROT IN? . . . WAIT, THAT'S A SILLY QUESTION
NOT AS MUCH AS YOU THINK; COME IN!
GIVEN THAT SHE'S PSYCHIC, I THOUGHT SHE WOULD HAVE COME OVER TO "RESCUE" ME AGAIN WHEN THE POWER WENT OUT
THE POWER'S OUT?
. . . WAIT, BUT YOU HAVE CANDLES?
RIGHT, I'M AN IDIOT
DON'T BLAME YOURSELF, WE WOULDN'T HAVE OUR DARK CHANTING CD ON EVEN IF WE HAD POWER
NOT SINCE I PUT IN "BEST OF QUEEN" BY MISTAKE
YOU CERTAINLY TAKE THIS OCCULT STUFF WELL; A LOT OF PEOPLE GET SORE AT SEEING MAGIC CIRCLES
WHAT CAN I SAY? I'M A DOG--I LIKE EXCITEMENT. ALSO, BARKING AT IT FROM A DISTANCE
TAROT CHOSE YOU WELL. THEN AGAIN, SHE HAS A LOT OF HELP
FROM THE SPIRITS, I KNOW
I MEAN THE DRAGON, ACTUALLY
DING
AREN'T YOU EVEN GOING TO ASK?
YEAH, WHY ARE WE IN AN ELEVATOR?
NO, ABOUT-- NEVERMIND

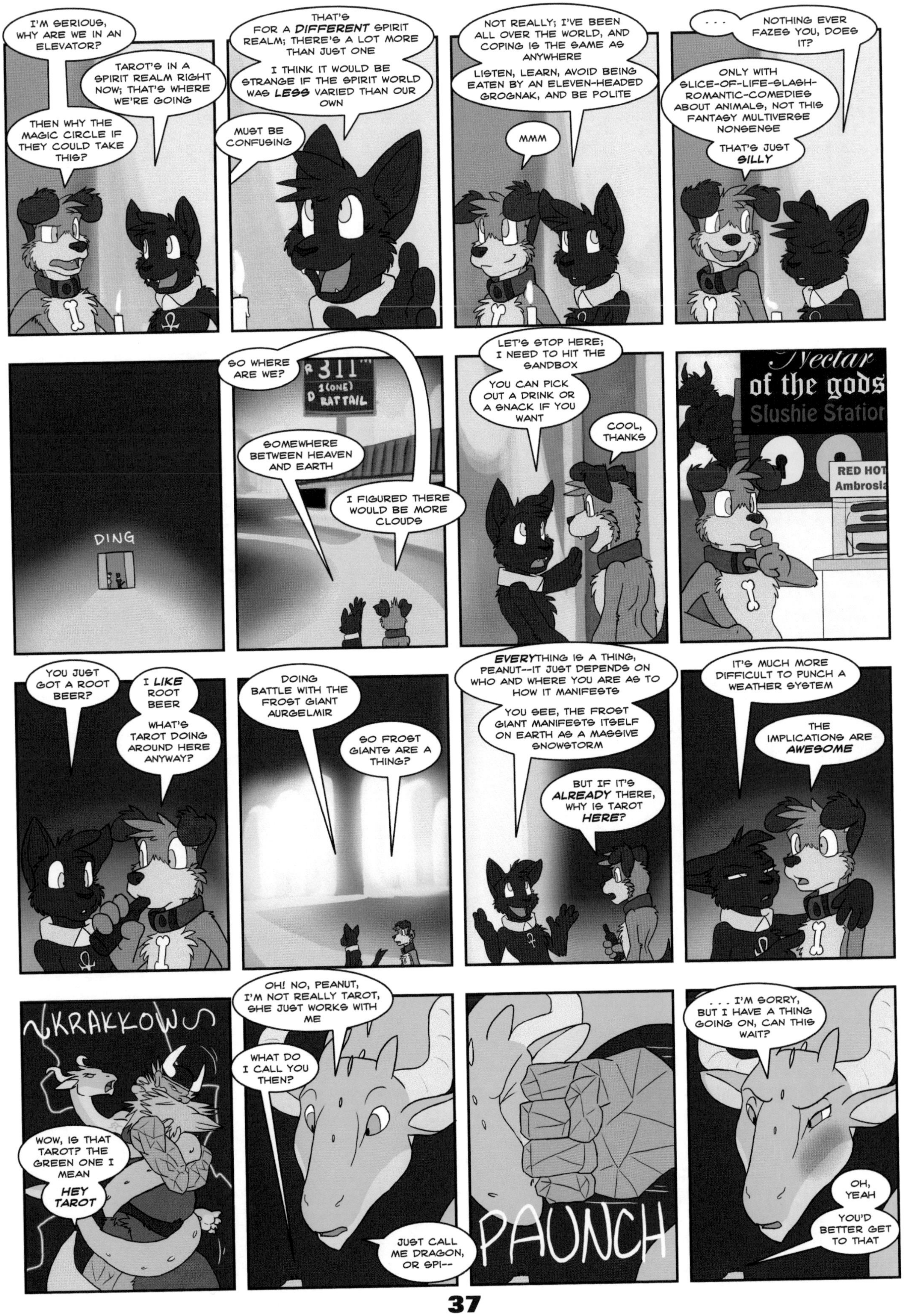
I'M SERIOUS, WHY ARE WE IN AN ELEVATOR?
TAROT'S IN A SPIRIT REALM RIGHT NOW; THAT'S WHERE WE'RE GOING
THEN WHY THE MAGIC CIRCLE IF THEY COULD TAKE THIS?
THAT'S FOR A DIFFERENT SPIRIT REALM; THERE'S A LOT MORE THAN JUST ONE
I THINK IT WOULD BE STRANGE IF THE SPIRIT WORLD WAS LESS VARIED THAN OUR OWN
MUST BE CONFUSING
NOT REALLY; I'VE BEEN ALL OVER THE WORLD, AND COPING IS THE SAME AS ANYWHERE
LISTEN, LEARN, AVOID BEING EATEN BY AN ELEVEN-HEADED GROGNAK, AND BE POLITE
MMM
. . .
NOTHING EVER FAZES YOU, DOES IT?
ONLY WITH SLICE-OF-LIFE-SLASH-ROMANTIC-COMEDIES ABOUT ANIMALS, NOT THIS FANTASY MULTIVERSE NONSENSE
THAT'S JUST SILLY
DING
SO WHERE ARE WE?
311
1 (ONE)
RATTAIL
SOMEWHERE BETWEEN HEAVEN AND EARTH
I FIGURED THERE WOULD BE MORE CLOUDS
LET'S STOP HERE; I NEED TO HIT THE SANDBOX
YOU CAN PICK OUT A DRINK OR A SNACK IF YOU WANT
COOL, THANKS
Nectar of the gods
Slushie Station
RED HOT
Ambrosia
YOU JUST GOT A ROOT BEER?
I LIKE ROOT BEER
WHAT'S TAROT DOING AROUND HERE ANYWAY?
DOING BATTLE WITH THE FROST GIANT AURGELMIR
SO FROST GIANTS ARE A THING?
EVERYTHING IS A THING, PEANUT--IT JUST DEPENDS ON WHO AND WHERE YOU ARE AS TO HOW IT MANIFESTS
YOU SEE, THE FROST GIANT MANIFESTS ITSELF ON EARTH AS A MASSIVE SNOWSTORM
BUT IF IT'S ALREADY THERE, WHY IS TAROT HERE?
IT'S MUCH MORE DIFFICULT TO PUNCH A WEATHER SYSTEM
THE IMPLICATIONS ARE AWESOME
KRAKKOW
WOW, IS THAT TAROT? THE GREEN ONE I MEAN
HEY TAROT
OH! NO, PEANUT, I'M NOT REALLY TAROT, SHE JUST WORKS WITH ME
WHAT DO I CALL YOU THEN?
JUST CALL ME DRAGON, OR SPI--
PAUNCH
. . . I'M SORRY, BUT I HAVE A THING GOING ON, CAN THIS WAIT?
OH, YEAH
YOU'D BETTER GET TO THAT

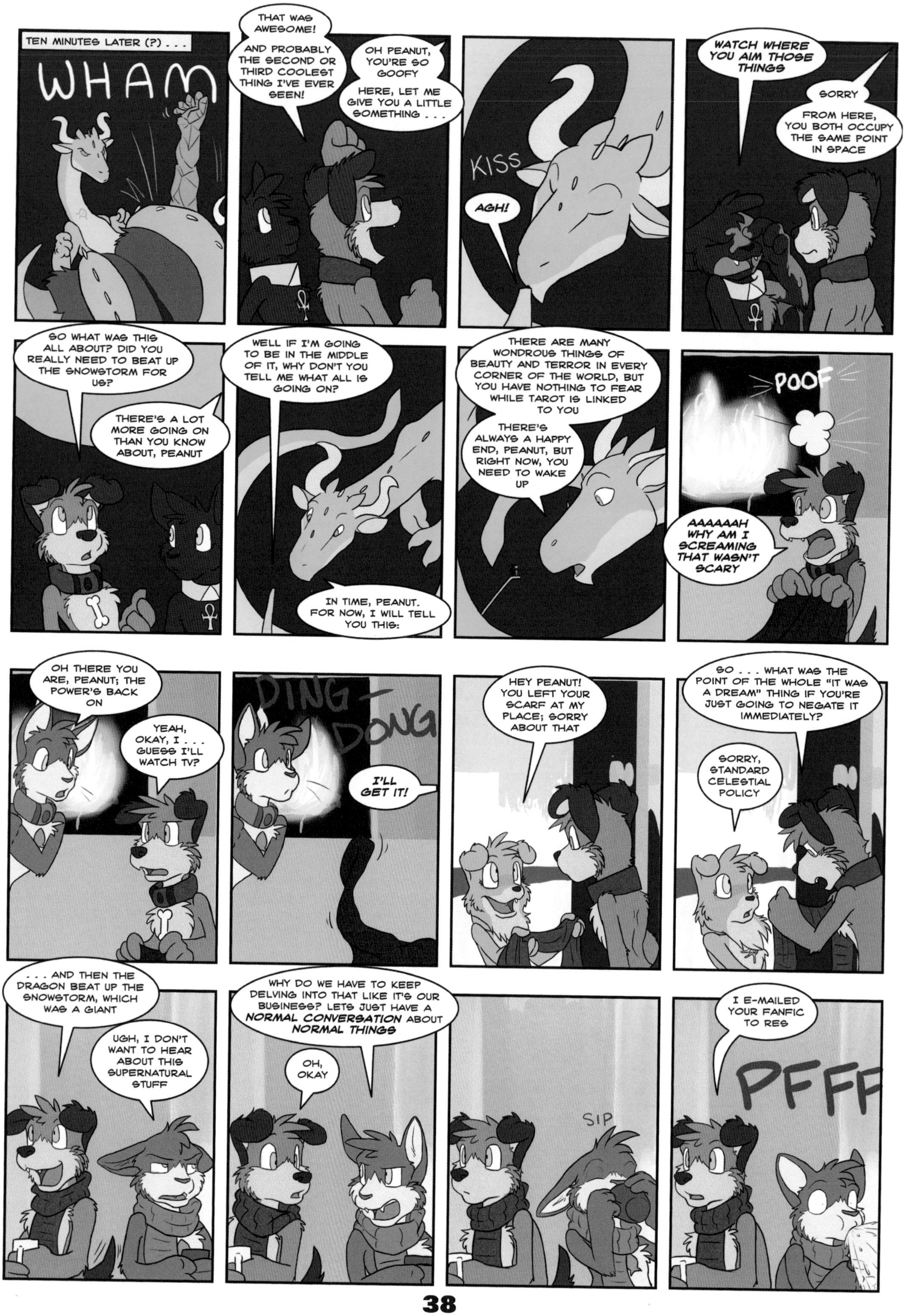
TEN MINUTES LATER (?) . . .
WHAM
THAT WAS AWESOME!
AND PROBABLY THE SECOND OR THIRD COOLEST THING I'VE EVER SEEN!
OH PEANUT, YOU'RE SO GOOFY
HERE, LET ME GIVE YOU A LITTLE SOMETHING . . .
KISS
AGH!
WATCH WHERE YOU AIM THOSE THINGS
SORRY
FROM HERE, YOU BOTH OCCUPY THE SAME POINT IN SPACE
SO WHAT WAS THIS ALL ABOUT? DID YOU REALLY NEED TO BEAT UP THE SNOWSTORM FOR US?
THERE'S A LOT MORE GOING ON THAN YOU KNOW ABOUT, PEANUT
WELL IF I'M GOING TO BE IN THE MIDDLE OF IT, WHY DON'T YOU TELL ME WHAT ALL IS GOING ON?
IN TIME, PEANUT. FOR NOW, I WILL TELL YOU THIS:
THERE ARE MANY WONDROUS THINGS OF BEAUTY AND TERROR IN EVERY CORNER OF THE WORLD, BUT YOU HAVE NOTHING TO FEAR WHILE TAROT IS LINKED TO YOU
THERE'S ALWAYS A HAPPY END, PEANUT, BUT RIGHT NOW, YOU NEED TO WAKE UP
POOF
AAAAAAH WHY AM I SCREAMING THAT WASN'T SCARY
OH THERE YOU ARE, PEANUT; THE POWER'S BACK ON
YEAH, OKAY, I . . . GUESS I'LL WATCH TV?
DING-DONG
I'LL GET IT!
HEY PEANUT! YOU LEFT YOUR SCARF AT MY PLACE; SORRY ABOUT THAT
SO . . . WHAT WAS THE POINT OF THE WHOLE "IT WAS A DREAM" THING IF YOU'RE JUST GOING TO NEGATE IT IMMEDIATELY?
SORRY, STANDARD CELESTIAL POLICY
. . . AND THEN THE DRAGON BEAT UP THE SNOWSTORM, WHICH WAS A GIANT
UGH, I DON'T WANT TO HEAR ABOUT THIS SUPERNATURAL STUFF
WHY DO WE HAVE TO KEEP DELVING INTO THAT LIKE IT'S OUR BUSINESS? LETS JUST HAVE A NORMAL CONVERSATION ABOUT NORMAL THINGS
OH, OKAY
SIP
I E-MAILED YOUR FANFIC TO RES
PFFF

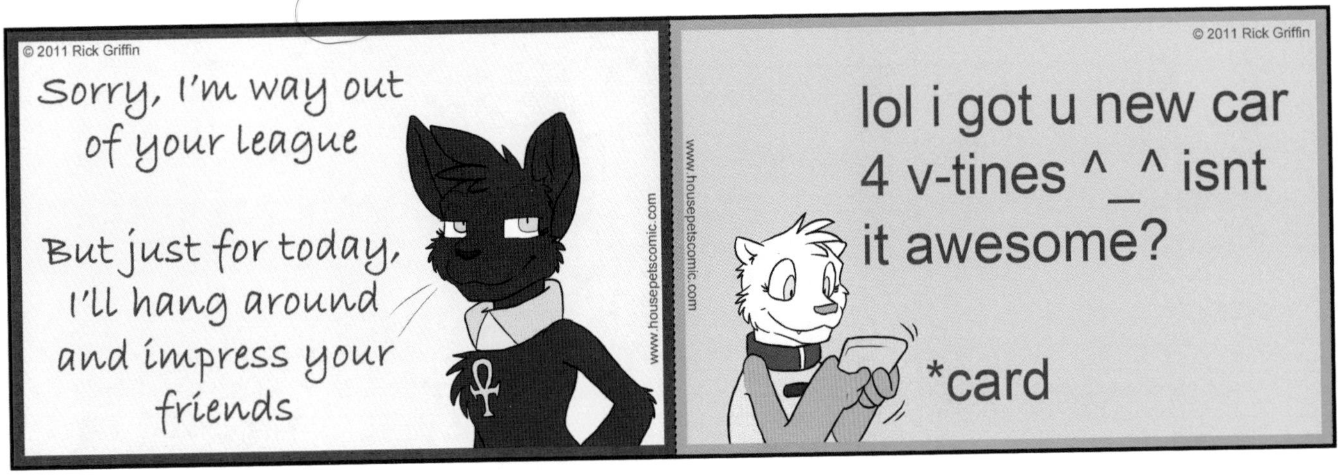
© 2011 Rick Griffin
Sorry, I'm way out of your league
But just for today, I'll hang around and impress your friends
www.housepetscomic.com
© 2011 Rick Griffin
www.housepetscomic.com
lol i got u new car 4 v-tines ^_^ isnt it awesome?
*card

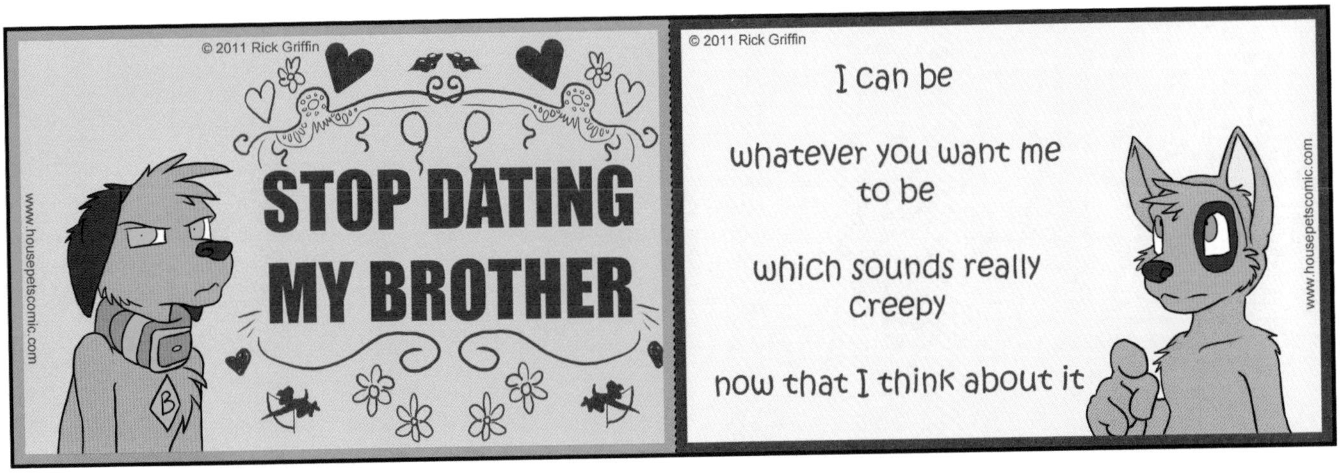
© 2011 Rick Griffin
www.housepetscomic.com
STOP DATING MY BROTHER
© 2011 Rick Griffin
I can be
whatever you want me to be
which sounds really creepy
now that I think about it
www.housepetscomic.com

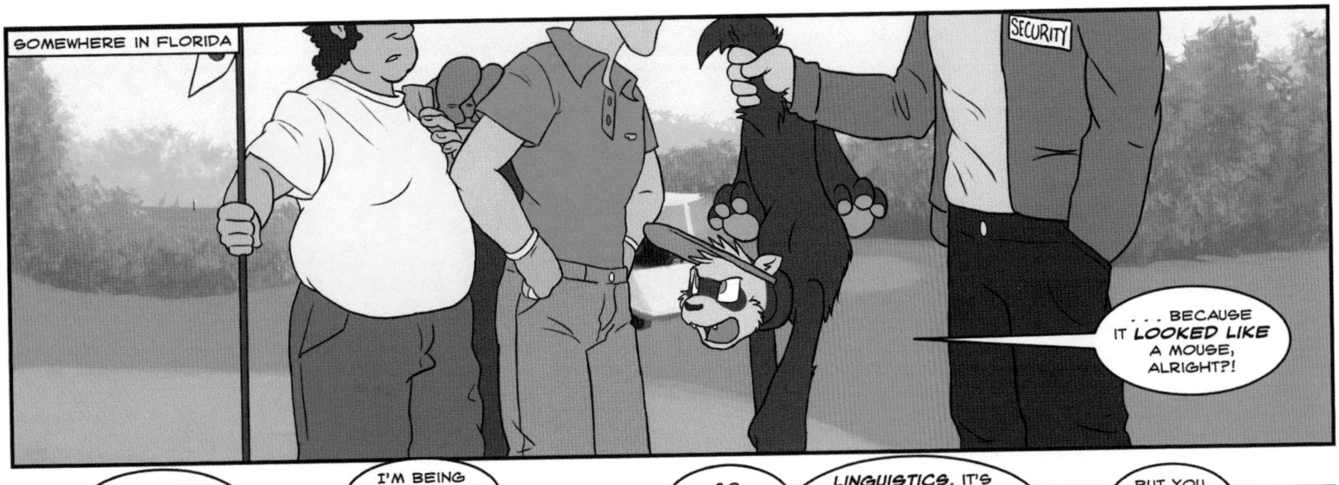
SOMEWHERE IN FLORIDA
SECURITY
. . . BECAUSE IT **LOOKED LIKE** A MOUSE, ALRIGHT?!

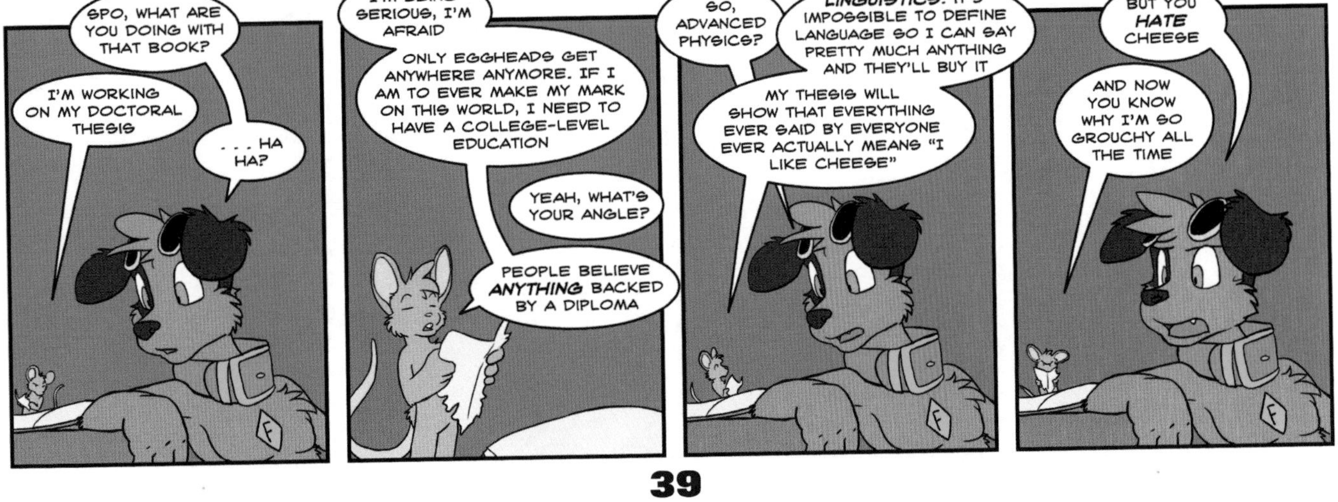
SPO, WHAT ARE YOU DOING WITH THAT BOOK?
I'M WORKING ON MY DOCTORAL THESIS
. . . HA HA?
I'M BEING SERIOUS, I'M AFRAID
ONLY EGGHEADS GET ANYWHERE ANYMORE. IF I AM TO EVER MAKE MY MARK ON THIS WORLD, I NEED TO HAVE A COLLEGE-LEVEL EDUCATION
YEAH, WHAT'S YOUR ANGLE?
PEOPLE BELIEVE **ANYTHING** BACKED BY A DIPLOMA
SO, ADVANCED PHYSICS?
LINGUISTICS. IT'S IMPOSSIBLE TO DEFINE LANGUAGE SO I CAN SAY PRETTY MUCH ANYTHING AND THEY'LL BUY IT
MY THESIS WILL SHOW THAT EVERYTHING EVER SAID BY EVERYONE EVER ACTUALLY MEANS "I LIKE CHEESE"
BUT YOU **HATE** CHEESE
AND NOW YOU KNOW WHY I'M SO GROUCHY ALL THE TIME

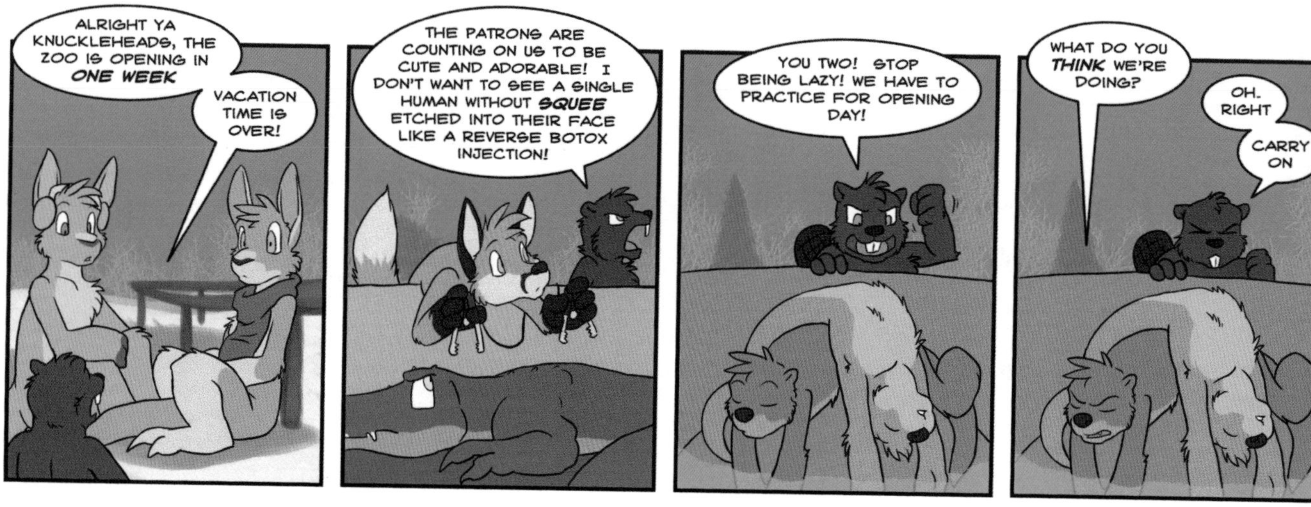
ALRIGHT YA KNUCKLEHEADS, THE ZOO IS OPENING IN ONE WEEK
VACATION TIME IS OVER!
THE PATRONS ARE COUNTING ON US TO BE CUTE AND ADORABLE! I DON'T WANT TO SEE A SINGLE HUMAN WITHOUT SQUEE ETCHED INTO THEIR FACE LIKE A REVERSE BOTOX INJECTION!
YOU TWO! STOP BEING LAZY! WE HAVE TO PRACTICE FOR OPENING DAY!
WHAT DO YOU THINK WE'RE DOING?
OH. RIGHT
CARRY ON

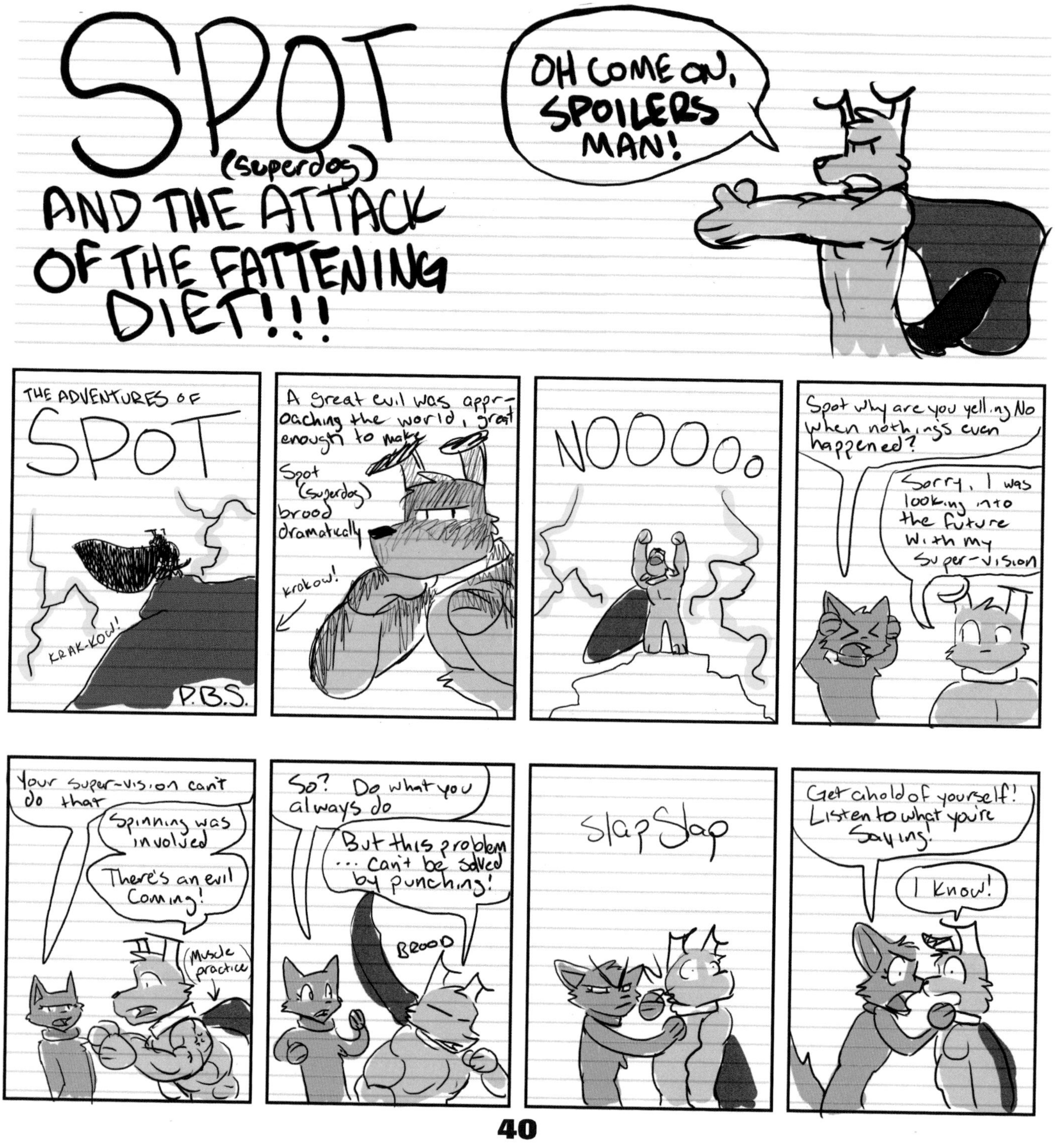
SPOT (superdog) AND THE ATTACK OF THE FATTENING DIET!!!
OH COME ON, SPOILERS MAN!
THE ADVENTURES OF SPOT
KRAK-KOW!
P.B.S.
A great evil was approaching the world, great enough to make Spot (superdog) brood dramatically
krokow!
NOOOOOo
Spot why are you yelling No when nothing's even happened?
Sorry, I was looking into the future With my Super-vision
Your super-vision can't do that
Spinning was involved
There's an evil Coming!
(Muscle practice)
So? Do what you always do
But this problem ... can't be solved by punching!
BROOD
Slap Slap
Get ahold of yourself! Listen to what you're Saying!
I know!

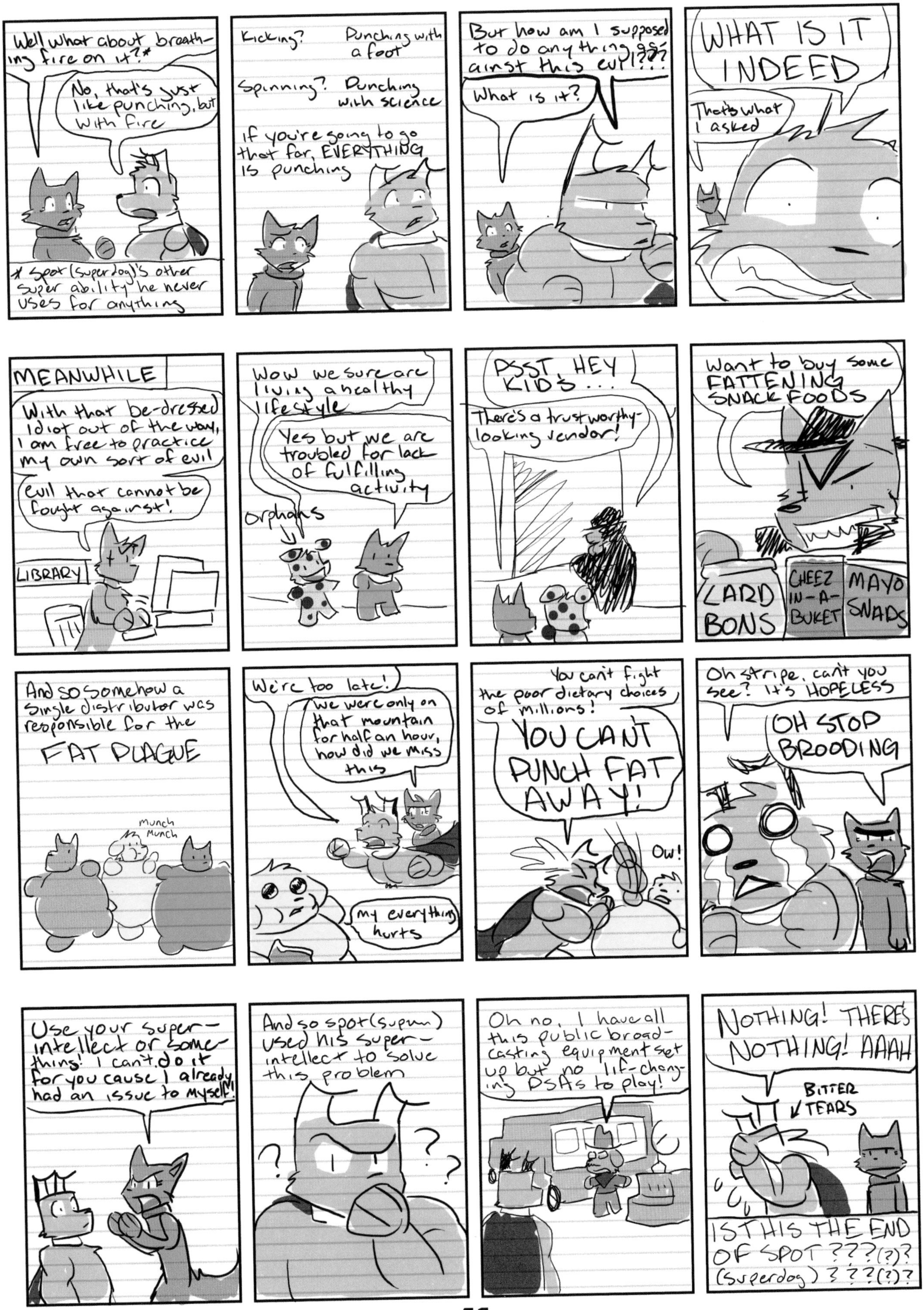
Well what about breathing fire on it?*
No, that's just like punching, but with fire
* Spot (superdog)'s other super ability he never uses for anything
Kicking?
Punching with a foot
Spinning?
Punching with science
If you're going to go that far, EVERYTHING is punching
But how am I supposed to do anything against this evil!???
What is it?
WHAT IS IT INDEED
That's what I asked
MEANWHILE
With that be-dressed idiot out of the way, I am free to practice my own sort of evil
evil that cannot be fought against!
LIBRARY
Wow we sure are living a healthy lifestyle
Yes but we are troubled for lack of fulfilling activity
orphans
PSST, HEY KIDS...
There's a trustworthy-looking vendor!
Want to buy some FATTENING SNACK FOODS
LARD BONS
CHEEZ IN-A-BUKET
MAYO SNADS
And so somehow a single distributor was responsible for the
FAT PLAGUE
munch munch
We're too late!
We were only on that mountain for half an hour, how did we miss this
my everything hurts
You can't fight the poor dietary choices of millions!
YOU CAN'T PUNCH FAT AWAY!
Ow!
Oh stripe, can't you see? It's HOPELESS
OH STOP BROODING
Use your super-intellect or something! I can't do it for you cause I already had an issue to myself!
And so spot (supm) used his super-intellect to solve this problem
Oh no, I have all this public broadcasting equipment set up but no lif-changing PSAs to play!
NOTHING! THERE'S NOTHING! AAAH
BITTER TEARS
IS THIS THE END OF SPOT???(?)? (Superdog)???(?)?

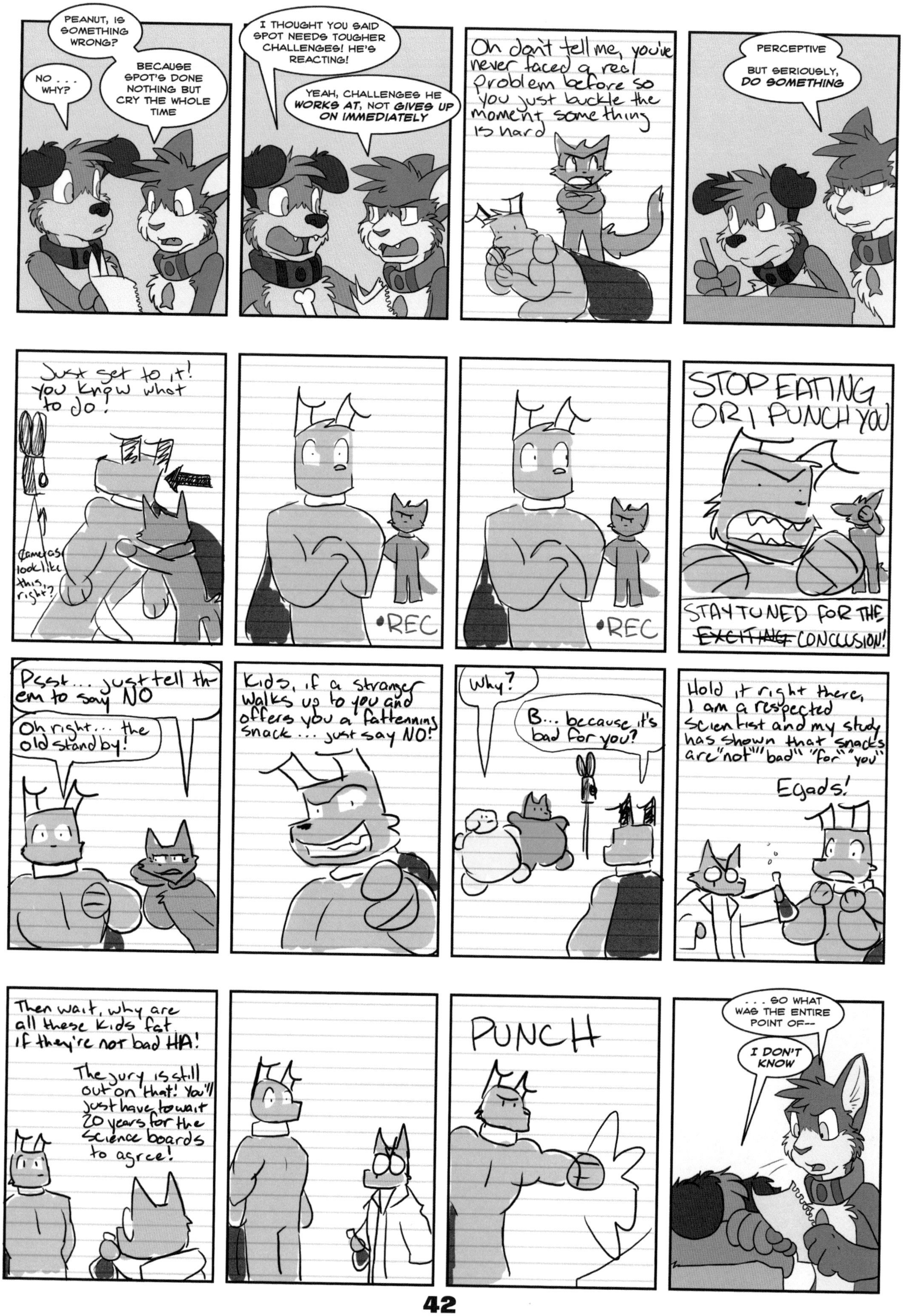

PEANUT, IS SOMETHING WRONG?
NO . . . WHY?
BECAUSE SPOT'S DONE NOTHING BUT CRY THE WHOLE TIME
I THOUGHT YOU SAID SPOT NEEDS TOUGHER CHALLENGES! HE'S REACTING!
YEAH, CHALLENGES HE ***WORKS AT,*** NOT ***GIVES UP ON IMMEDIATELY***
Oh don't tell me, you've never faced a real problem before so you just buckle the moment something is hard
PERCEPTIVE
BUT SERIOUSLY, ***DO SOMETHING***
Just get to it! you know what to do!
Cameras look like this, right?
•REC
•REC
STOP EATING OR I PUNCH YOU
STAY TUNED FOR THE ~~EXCITING~~ CONCLUSION!
Psst... just tell them to say NO
Oh right... the old stand by!
Kids, if a stranger walks up to you and offers you a fattenning snack... just say NO!
Why?
B... because it's bad for you?
Hold it right there, I am a respected scientist and my study has shown that snacks are "not" "bad" "for" "you"
Egads!
Then wait, why are all these kids fat if they're not bad HA!
The jury is still out on that! You'll just have to wait 20 years for the science boards to agree!
PUNCH
. . . SO WHAT WAS THE ENTIRE POINT OF--
I DON'T KNOW

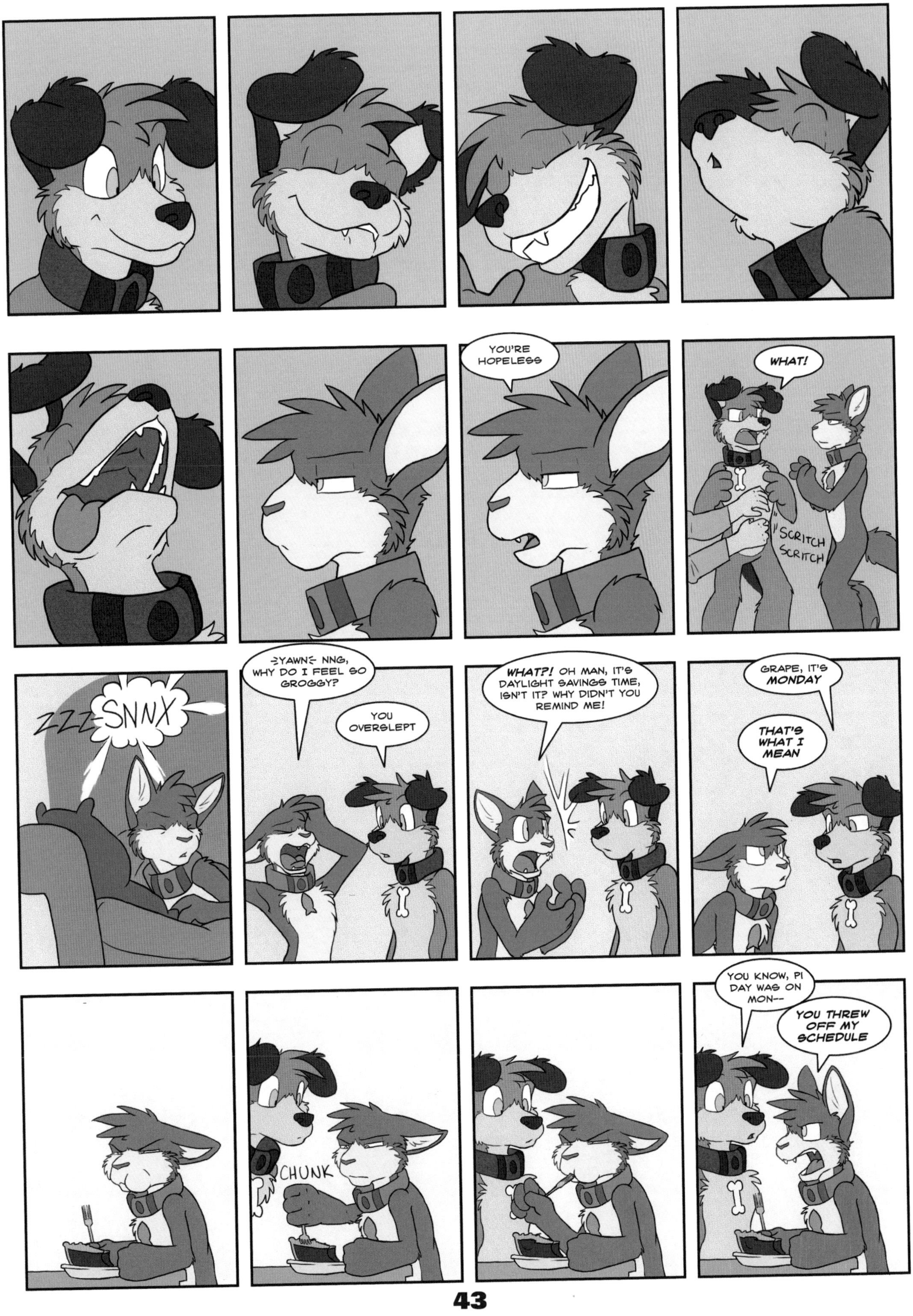
YOU'RE HOPELESS
WHAT!
SCRITCH SCRITCH
ZZZ SNNX
=YAWN= NNG, WHY DO I FEEL SO GROGGY?
YOU OVERSLEPT
WHAT?! OH MAN, IT'S DAYLIGHT SAVINGS TIME, ISN'T IT? WHY DIDN'T YOU REMIND ME!
GRAPE, IT'S MONDAY
THAT'S WHAT I MEAN
CHUNK
YOU KNOW, PI DAY WAS ON MON--
YOU THREW OFF MY SCHEDULE

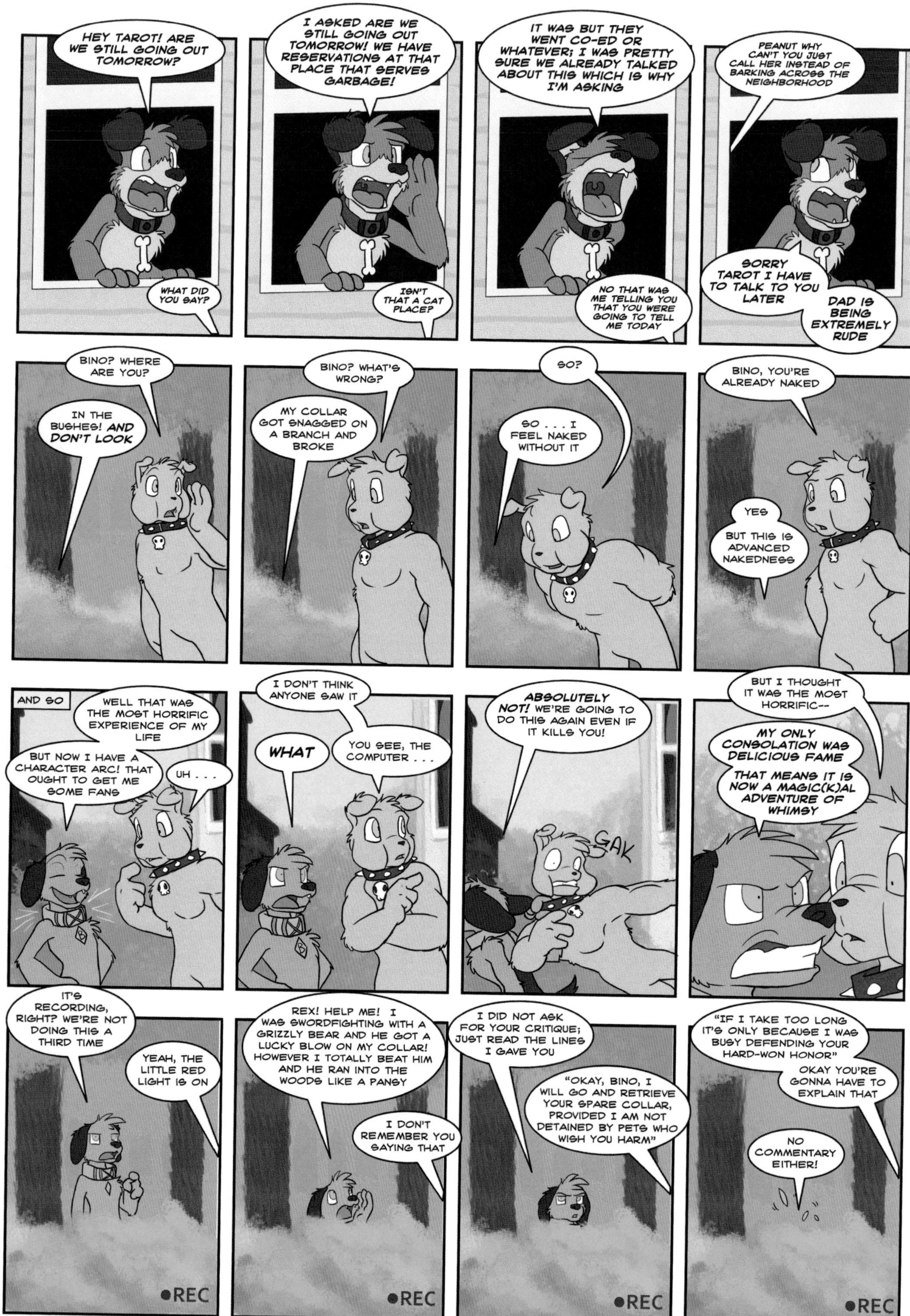
HEY TAROT! ARE WE STILL GOING OUT TOMORROW?
WHAT DID YOU SAY?
I ASKED ARE WE STILL GOING OUT TOMORROW! WE HAVE RESERVATIONS AT THAT PLACE THAT SERVES GARBAGE!
ISN'T THAT A CAT PLACE?
IT WAS BUT THEY WENT CO-ED OR WHATEVER; I WAS PRETTY SURE WE ALREADY TALKED ABOUT THIS WHICH IS WHY I'M ASKING
NO THAT WAS ME TELLING YOU THAT YOU WERE GOING TO TELL ME TODAY
PEANUT WHY CAN'T YOU JUST CALL HER INSTEAD OF BARKING ACROSS THE NEIGHBORHOOD
SORRY TAROT I HAVE TO TALK TO YOU LATER
DAD IS BEING EXTREMELY RUDE
BINO? WHERE ARE YOU?
IN THE BUSHES! AND DON'T LOOK
BINO? WHAT'S WRONG?
MY COLLAR GOT SNAGGED ON A BRANCH AND BROKE
SO?
SO . . . I FEEL NAKED WITHOUT IT
BINO, YOU'RE ALREADY NAKED
YES
BUT THIS IS ADVANCED NAKEDNESS
AND SO
WELL THAT WAS THE MOST HORRIFIC EXPERIENCE OF MY LIFE
BUT NOW I HAVE A CHARACTER ARC! THAT OUGHT TO GET ME SOME FANS
UH . . .
I DON'T THINK ANYONE SAW IT
WHAT
YOU SEE, THE COMPUTER . . .
ABSOLUTELY NOT! WE'RE GOING TO DO THIS AGAIN EVEN IF IT KILLS YOU!
GAK
BUT I THOUGHT IT WAS THE MOST HORRIFIC--
MY ONLY CONSOLATION WAS DELICIOUS FAME
THAT MEANS IT IS NOW A MAGIC(K)AL ADVENTURE OF WHIMSY
IT'S RECORDING, RIGHT? WE'RE NOT DOING THIS A THIRD TIME
YEAH, THE LITTLE RED LIGHT IS ON
●REC
REX! HELP ME! I WAS SWORDFIGHTING WITH A GRIZZLY BEAR AND HE GOT A LUCKY BLOW ON MY COLLAR! HOWEVER I TOTALLY BEAT HIM AND HE RAN INTO THE WOODS LIKE A PANSY
I DON'T REMEMBER YOU SAYING THAT
●REC
I DID NOT ASK FOR YOUR CRITIQUE; JUST READ THE LINES I GAVE YOU
"OKAY, BINO, I WILL GO AND RETRIEVE YOUR SPARE COLLAR, PROVIDED I AM NOT DETAINED BY PETS WHO WISH YOU HARM"
●REC
"IF I TAKE TOO LONG IT'S ONLY BECAUSE I WAS BUSY DEFENDING YOUR HARD-WON HONOR"
OKAY YOU'RE GONNA HAVE TO EXPLAIN THAT
NO COMMENTARY EITHER!
●REC

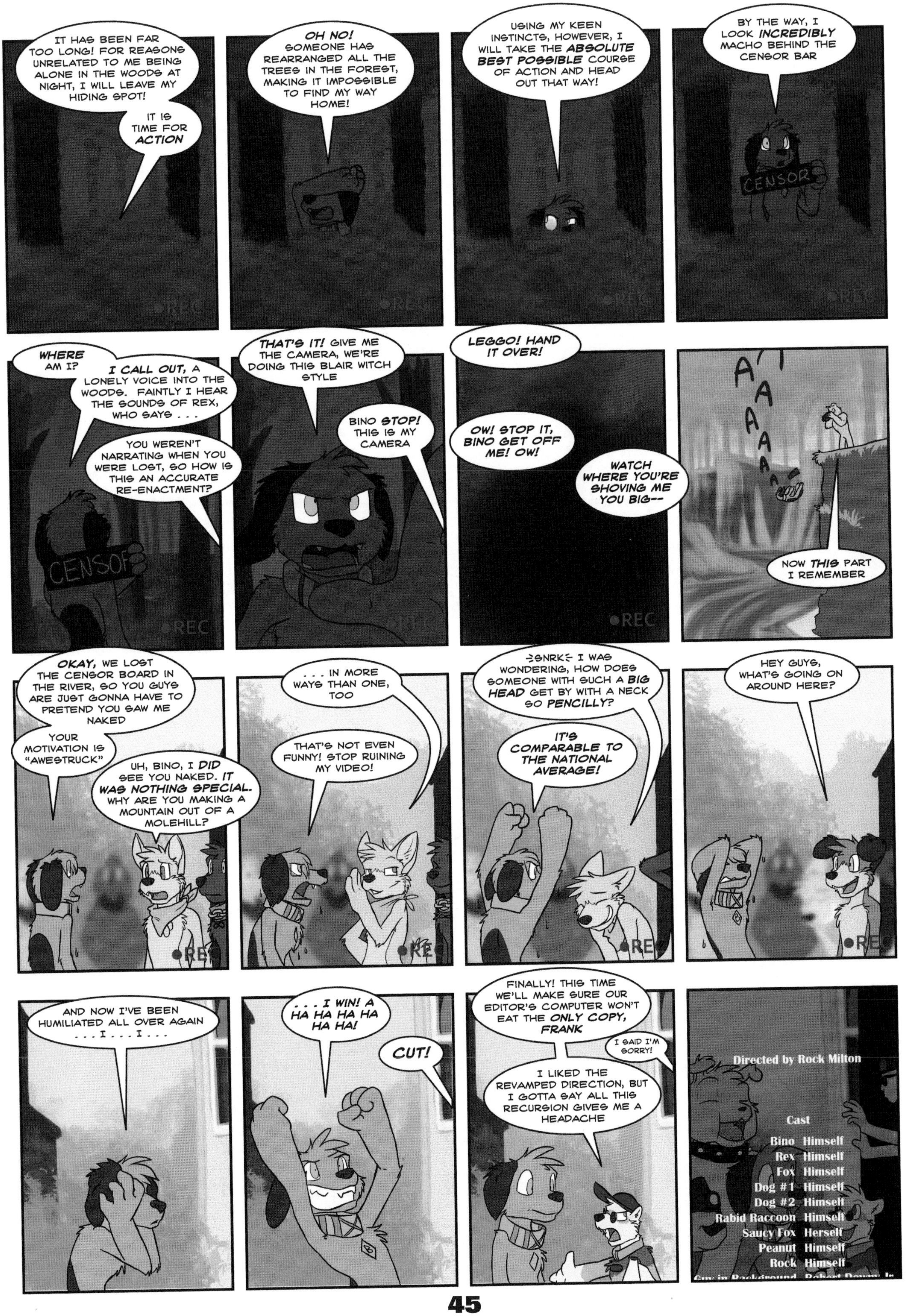

IT HAS BEEN FAR TOO LONG! FOR REASONS UNRELATED TO ME BEING ALONE IN THE WOODS AT NIGHT, I WILL LEAVE MY HIDING SPOT!
IT IS TIME FOR ACTION
●REC
OH NO! SOMEONE HAS REARRANGED ALL THE TREES IN THE FOREST, MAKING IT IMPOSSIBLE TO FIND MY WAY HOME!
●REC
USING MY KEEN INSTINCTS, HOWEVER, I WILL TAKE THE ABSOLUTE BEST POSSIBLE COURSE OF ACTION AND HEAD OUT THAT WAY!
●REC
BY THE WAY, I LOOK INCREDIBLY MACHO BEHIND THE CENSOR BAR
CENSOR
●REC
WHERE AM I?
I CALL OUT, A LONELY VOICE INTO THE WOODS. FAINTLY I HEAR THE SOUNDS OF REX, WHO SAYS . . .
YOU WEREN'T NARRATING WHEN YOU WERE LOST, SO HOW IS THIS AN ACCURATE RE-ENACTMENT?
CENSOF
●REC
THAT'S IT! GIVE ME THE CAMERA, WE'RE DOING THIS BLAIR WITCH STYLE
BINO STOP! THIS IS MY CAMERA
LEGGO! HAND IT OVER!
OW! STOP IT, BINO GET OFF ME! OW!
WATCH WHERE YOU'RE SHOVING ME YOU BIG--
●REC
A'AAAAAA
NOW THIS PART I REMEMBER
OKAY, WE LOST THE CENSOR BOARD IN THE RIVER, SO YOU GUYS ARE JUST GONNA HAVE TO PRETEND YOU SAW ME NAKED
YOUR MOTIVATION IS "AWESTRUCK"
UH, BINO, I DID SEE YOU NAKED. IT WAS NOTHING SPECIAL. WHY ARE YOU MAKING A MOUNTAIN OUT OF A MOLEHILL?
●REC
. . . IN MORE WAYS THAN ONE, TOO
THAT'S NOT EVEN FUNNY! STOP RUINING MY VIDEO!
●REC
=SNRK= I WAS WONDERING, HOW DOES SOMEONE WITH SUCH A BIG HEAD GET BY WITH A NECK SO PENCILLY?
IT'S COMPARABLE TO THE NATIONAL AVERAGE!
●REC
HEY GUYS, WHAT'S GOING ON AROUND HERE?
●REC
AND NOW I'VE BEEN HUMILIATED ALL OVER AGAIN . . . I . . . I . . .
. . . I WIN! A HA HA HA HA HA HA!
CUT!
FINALLY! THIS TIME WE'LL MAKE SURE OUR EDITOR'S COMPUTER WON'T EAT THE ONLY COPY, FRANK
I SAID I'M SORRY!
I LIKED THE REVAMPED DIRECTION, BUT I GOTTA SAY ALL THIS RECURSION GIVES ME A HEADACHE
Directed by Rock Milton
Cast
Bino Himself
Rex Himself
Fox Himself
Dog #1 Himself
Dog #2 Himself
Rabid Raccoon Himself
Saucy Fox Herself
Peanut Himself
Rock Himself

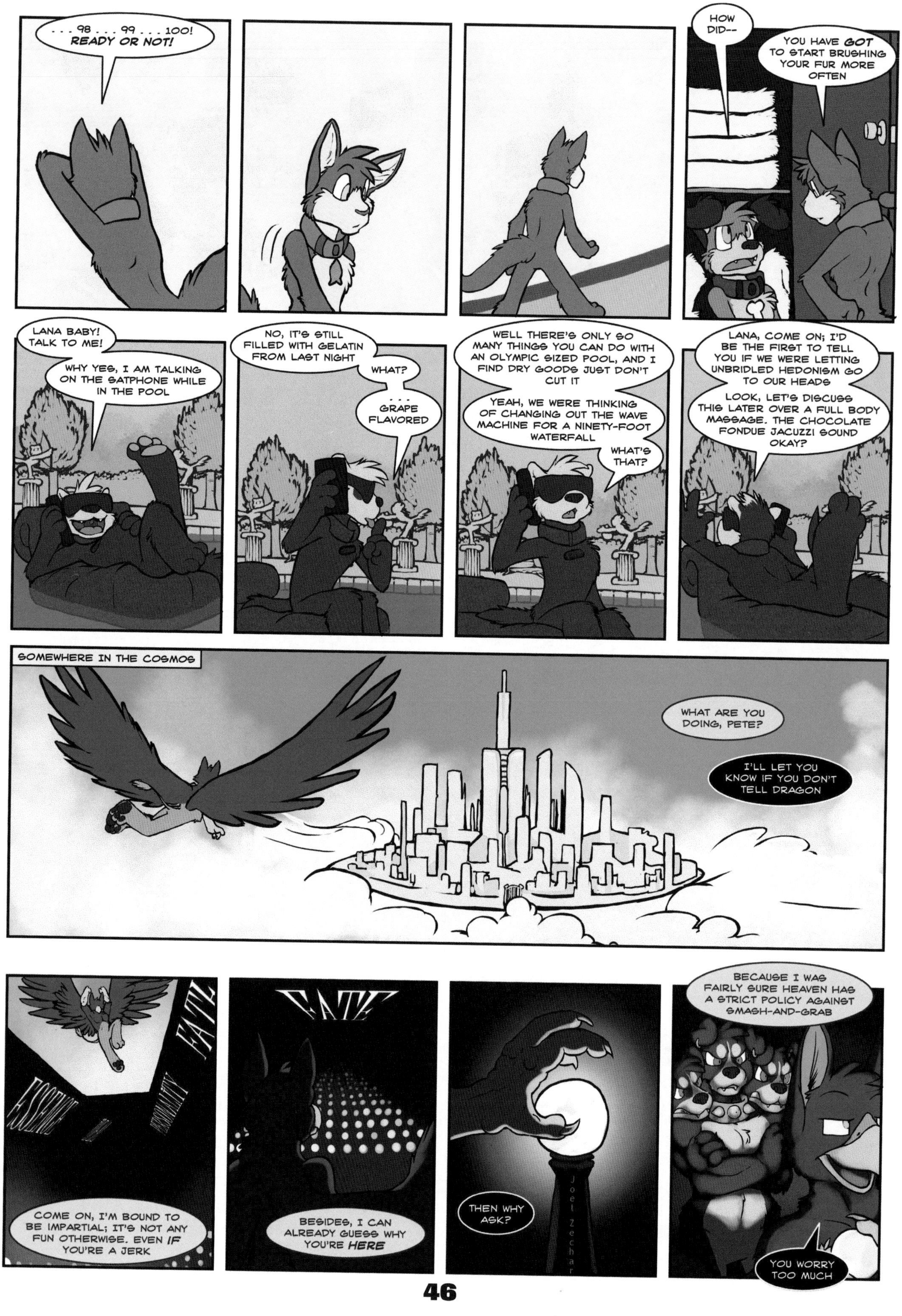
. . . 98 . . . 99 . . . 100! READY OR NOT!
HOW DID--
YOU HAVE GOT TO START BRUSHING YOUR FUR MORE OFTEN
LANA BABY! TALK TO ME!
WHY YES, I AM TALKING ON THE SATPHONE WHILE IN THE POOL
NO, IT'S STILL FILLED WITH GELATIN FROM LAST NIGHT
WHAT?
. . . GRAPE FLAVORED
WELL THERE'S ONLY SO MANY THINGS YOU CAN DO WITH AN OLYMPIC SIZED POOL, AND I FIND DRY GOODS JUST DON'T CUT IT
YEAH, WE WERE THINKING OF CHANGING OUT THE WAVE MACHINE FOR A NINETY-FOOT WATERFALL
WHAT'S THAT?
LANA, COME ON; I'D BE THE FIRST TO TELL YOU IF WE WERE LETTING UNBRIDLED HEDONISM GO TO OUR HEADS
LOOK, LET'S DISCUSS THIS LATER OVER A FULL BODY MASSAGE. THE CHOCOLATE FONDUE JACUZZI SOUND OKAY?
SOMEWHERE IN THE COSMOS
WHAT ARE YOU DOING, PETE?
I'LL LET YOU KNOW IF YOU DON'T TELL DRAGON
FATE
COME ON, I'M BOUND TO BE IMPARTIAL; IT'S NOT ANY FUN OTHERWISE. EVEN IF YOU'RE A JERK
BESIDES, I CAN ALREADY GUESS WHY YOU'RE HERE
THEN WHY ASK?
Joel Zechar
BECAUSE I WAS FAIRLY SURE HEAVEN HAS A STRICT POLICY AGAINST SMASH-AND-GRAB
YOU WORRY TOO MUCH

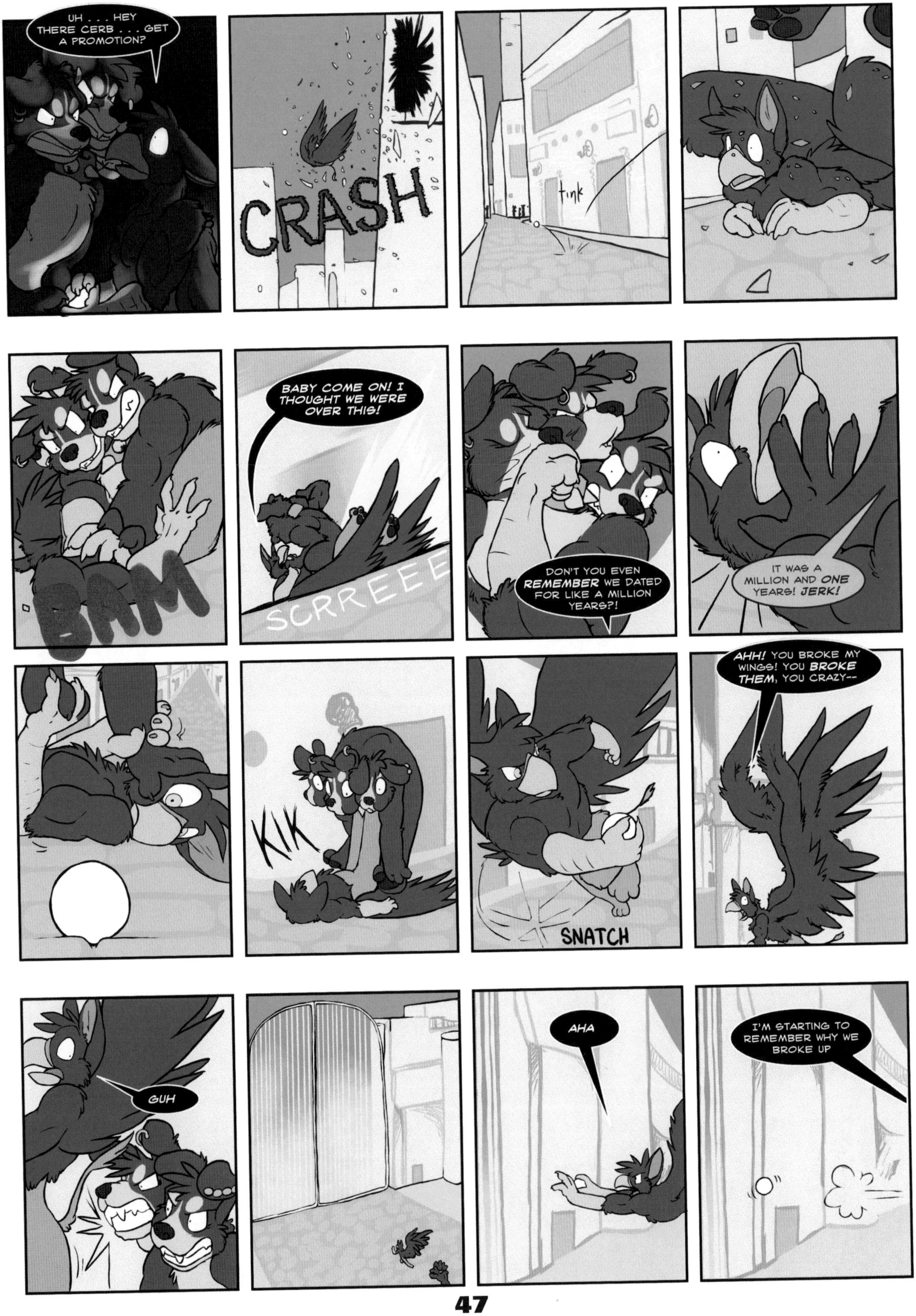
UH . . . HEY THERE CERB . . . GET A PROMOTION?
CRASH
tink
BAM
BABY COME ON! I THOUGHT WE WERE OVER THIS!
SCRREEE
DON'T YOU EVEN REMEMBER WE DATED FOR LIKE A MILLION YEARS?!
IT WAS A MILLION AND ONE YEARS! JERK!
KIK
SNATCH
AHH! YOU BROKE MY WINGS! YOU BROKE THEM, YOU CRAZY--
GUH
AHA
I'M STARTING TO REMEMBER WHY WE BROKE UP

LET GO! THE FATE IS GOING TO--
tink
NO! LET GO! YOU DON'T KNOW WHAT YOU'RE DOING!
OW! SON OF A CHARMING YOUNG WOMAN
WHAT HAPPENED?
THIS THING HIT ME ON THE HEAD . . .
HUH, LOOKS LIKE A SEMI-FANCY SPORTS WATCH. I WONDER WHAT KIND IT IS
6:04 PM
JOEL ZECHARIAH ROBINSON
ON SECOND THOUGHT, WHAT DOES A DOG NEED A WATCH FOR?
YOU COULD BECOME A WATCH--
HA HA SHUT UP

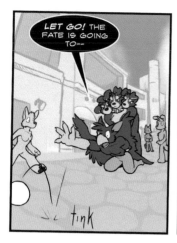

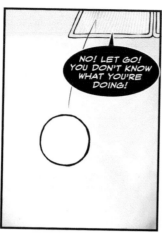

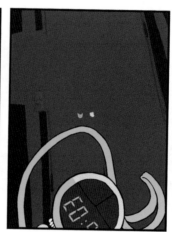

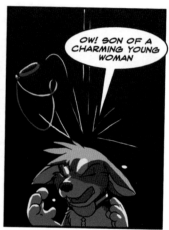

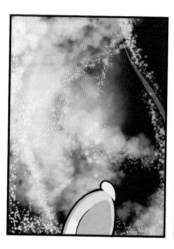

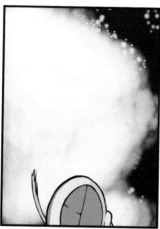

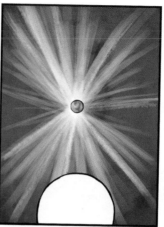

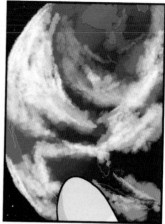

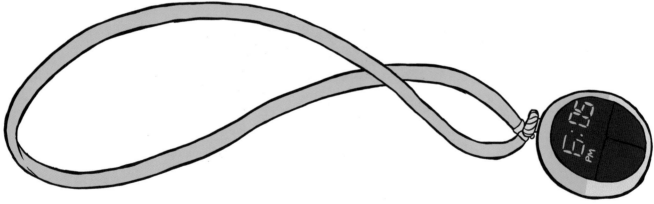

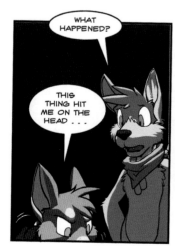

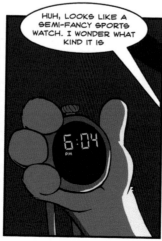

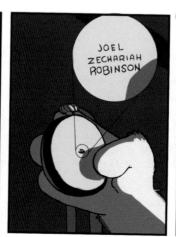

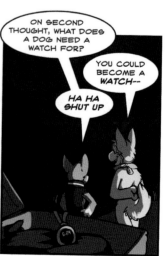

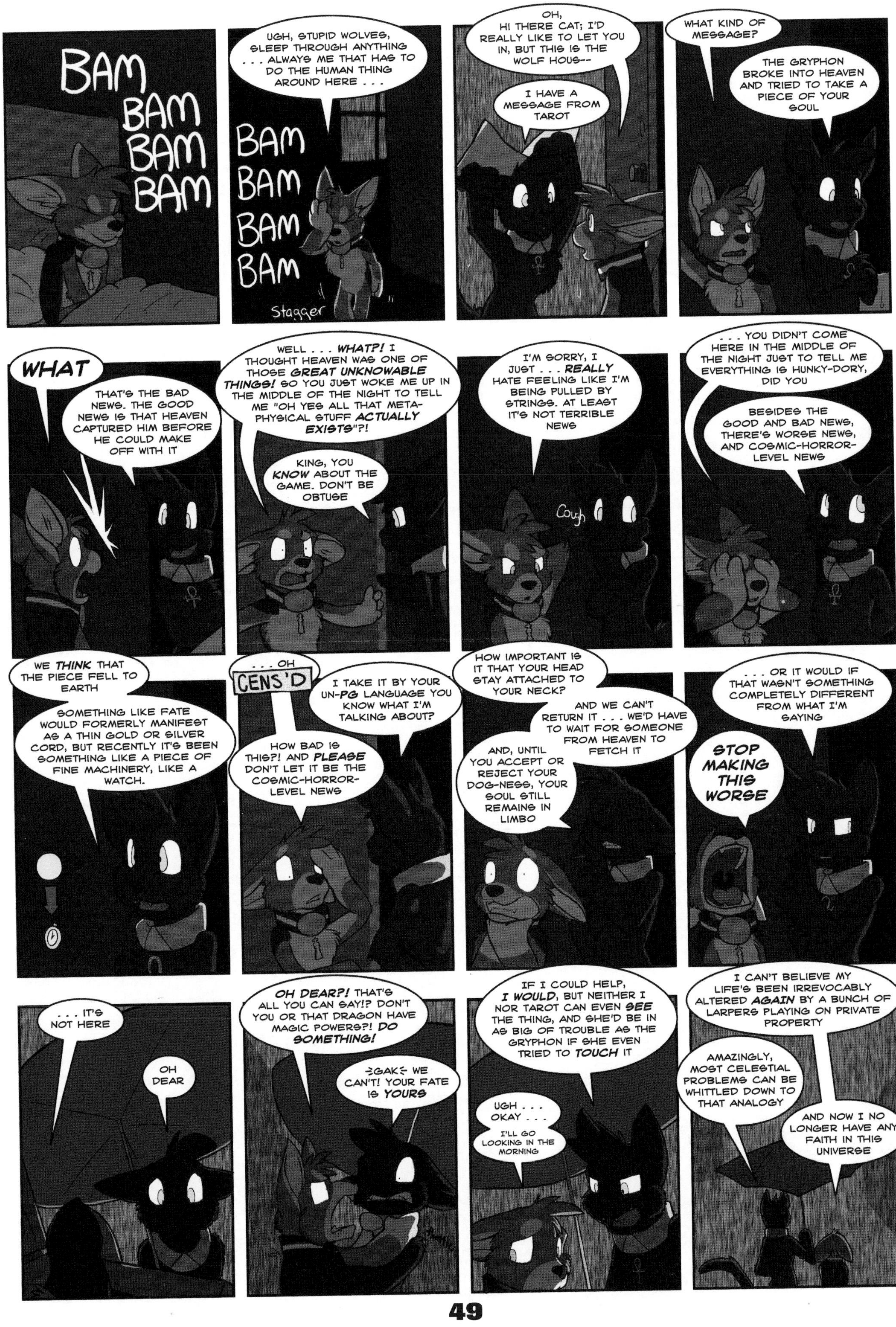

BAM BAM BAM BAM
UGH, STUPID WOLVES, SLEEP THROUGH ANYTHING . . . ALWAYS ME THAT HAS TO DO THE HUMAN THING AROUND HERE . . .
BAM BAM BAM BAM
stagger
OH, HI THERE CAT; I'D REALLY LIKE TO LET YOU IN, BUT THIS IS THE WOLF HOUS--
I HAVE A MESSAGE FROM TAROT
WHAT KIND OF MESSAGE?
THE GRYPHON BROKE INTO HEAVEN AND TRIED TO TAKE A PIECE OF YOUR SOUL
WHAT
THAT'S THE BAD NEWS. THE GOOD NEWS IS THAT HEAVEN CAPTURED HIM BEFORE HE COULD MAKE OFF WITH IT
WELL . . . WHAT?! I THOUGHT HEAVEN WAS ONE OF THOSE GREAT UNKNOWABLE THINGS! SO YOU JUST WOKE ME UP IN THE MIDDLE OF THE NIGHT TO TELL ME "OH YES ALL THAT META-PHYSICAL STUFF ACTUALLY EXISTS"?!
KING, YOU KNOW ABOUT THE GAME. DON'T BE OBTUSE
I'M SORRY, I JUST . . . REALLY HATE FEELING LIKE I'M BEING PULLED BY STRINGS. AT LEAST IT'S NOT TERRIBLE NEWS
Cough
. . . YOU DIDN'T COME HERE IN THE MIDDLE OF THE NIGHT JUST TO TELL ME EVERYTHING IS HUNKY-DORY, DID YOU
BESIDES THE GOOD AND BAD NEWS, THERE'S WORSE NEWS, AND COSMIC-HORROR-LEVEL NEWS
WE THINK THAT THE PIECE FELL TO EARTH
SOMETHING LIKE FATE WOULD FORMERLY MANIFEST AS A THIN GOLD OR SILVER CORD, BUT RECENTLY IT'S BEEN SOMETHING LIKE A PIECE OF FINE MACHINERY, LIKE A WATCH.
. . . OH CENS'D
I TAKE IT BY YOUR UN-PG LANGUAGE YOU KNOW WHAT I'M TALKING ABOUT?
HOW BAD IS THIS?! AND PLEASE DON'T LET IT BE THE COSMIC-HORROR-LEVEL NEWS
HOW IMPORTANT IS IT THAT YOUR HEAD STAY ATTACHED TO YOUR NECK?
AND WE CAN'T RETURN IT . . . WE'D HAVE TO WAIT FOR SOMEONE FROM HEAVEN TO FETCH IT
AND, UNTIL YOU ACCEPT OR REJECT YOUR DOG-NESS, YOUR SOUL STILL REMAINS IN LIMBO
. . . OR IT WOULD IF THAT WASN'T SOMETHING COMPLETELY DIFFERENT FROM WHAT I'M SAYING
STOP MAKING THIS WORSE
. . . IT'S NOT HERE
OH DEAR
OH DEAR?! THAT'S ALL YOU CAN SAY!? DON'T YOU OR THAT DRAGON HAVE MAGIC POWERS?! DO SOMETHING!
GAK WE CAN'T! YOUR FATE IS YOURS
IF I COULD HELP, I WOULD, BUT NEITHER I NOR TAROT CAN EVEN SEE THE THING, AND SHE'D BE IN AS BIG OF TROUBLE AS THE GRYPHON IF SHE EVEN TRIED TO TOUCH IT
UGH . . . OKAY . . .
I'LL GO LOOKING IN THE MORNING
I CAN'T BELIEVE MY LIFE'S BEEN IRREVOCABLY ALTERED AGAIN BY A BUNCH OF LARPERS PLAYING ON PRIVATE PROPERTY
AMAZINGLY, MOST CELESTIAL PROBLEMS CAN BE WHITTLED DOWN TO THAT ANALOGY
AND NOW I NO LONGER HAVE ANY FAITH IN THIS UNIVERSE

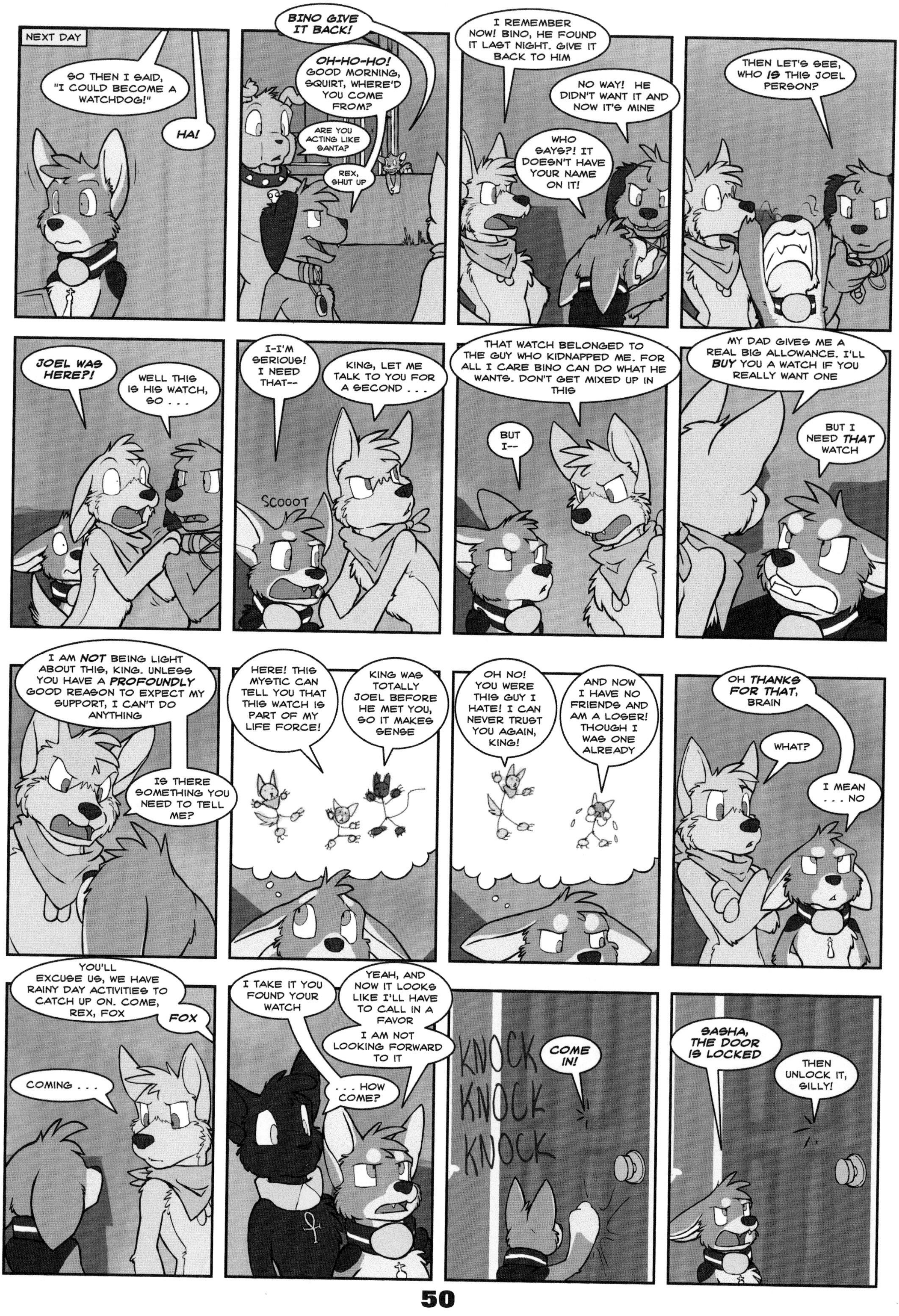
NEXT DAY
SO THEN I SAID, "I COULD BECOME A WATCHDOG!"
HA!
BINO GIVE IT BACK!
OH-HO-HO! GOOD MORNING, SQUIRT, WHERE'D YOU COME FROM?
ARE YOU ACTING LIKE SANTA?
REX, SHUT UP
I REMEMBER NOW! BINO, HE FOUND IT LAST NIGHT. GIVE IT BACK TO HIM
NO WAY! HE DIDN'T WANT IT AND NOW IT'S MINE
WHO SAYS?! IT DOESN'T HAVE YOUR NAME ON IT!
THEN LET'S SEE, WHO IS THIS JOEL PERSON?
JOEL WAS HERE?!
WELL THIS IS HIS WATCH, SO . . .
I-I'M SERIOUS! I NEED THAT--
KING, LET ME TALK TO YOU FOR A SECOND . . .
SCOOOT
THAT WATCH BELONGED TO THE GUY WHO KIDNAPPED ME. FOR ALL I CARE BINO CAN DO WHAT HE WANTS. DON'T GET MIXED UP IN THIS
BUT I--
MY DAD GIVES ME A REAL BIG ALLOWANCE. I'LL BUY YOU A WATCH IF YOU REALLY WANT ONE
BUT I NEED THAT WATCH
I AM NOT BEING LIGHT ABOUT THIS, KING. UNLESS YOU HAVE A PROFOUNDLY GOOD REASON TO EXPECT MY SUPPORT, I CAN'T DO ANYTHING
IS THERE SOMETHING YOU NEED TO TELL ME?
HERE! THIS MYSTIC CAN TELL YOU THAT THIS WATCH IS PART OF MY LIFE FORCE!
KING WAS TOTALLY JOEL BEFORE HE MET YOU, SO IT MAKES SENSE
OH NO! YOU WERE THIS GUY I HATE! I CAN NEVER TRUST YOU AGAIN, KING!
AND NOW I HAVE NO FRIENDS AND AM A LOSER! THOUGH I WAS ONE ALREADY
OH THANKS FOR THAT, BRAIN
WHAT?
I MEAN . . . NO
YOU'LL EXCUSE US, WE HAVE RAINY DAY ACTIVITIES TO CATCH UP ON. COME, REX, FOX
FOX
COMING . . .
I TAKE IT YOU FOUND YOUR WATCH
YEAH, AND NOW IT LOOKS LIKE I'LL HAVE TO CALL IN A FAVOR
I AM NOT LOOKING FORWARD TO IT
. . . HOW COME?
KNOCK KNOCK KNOCK
COME IN!
SASHA, THE DOOR IS LOCKED
THEN UNLOCK IT, SILLY!

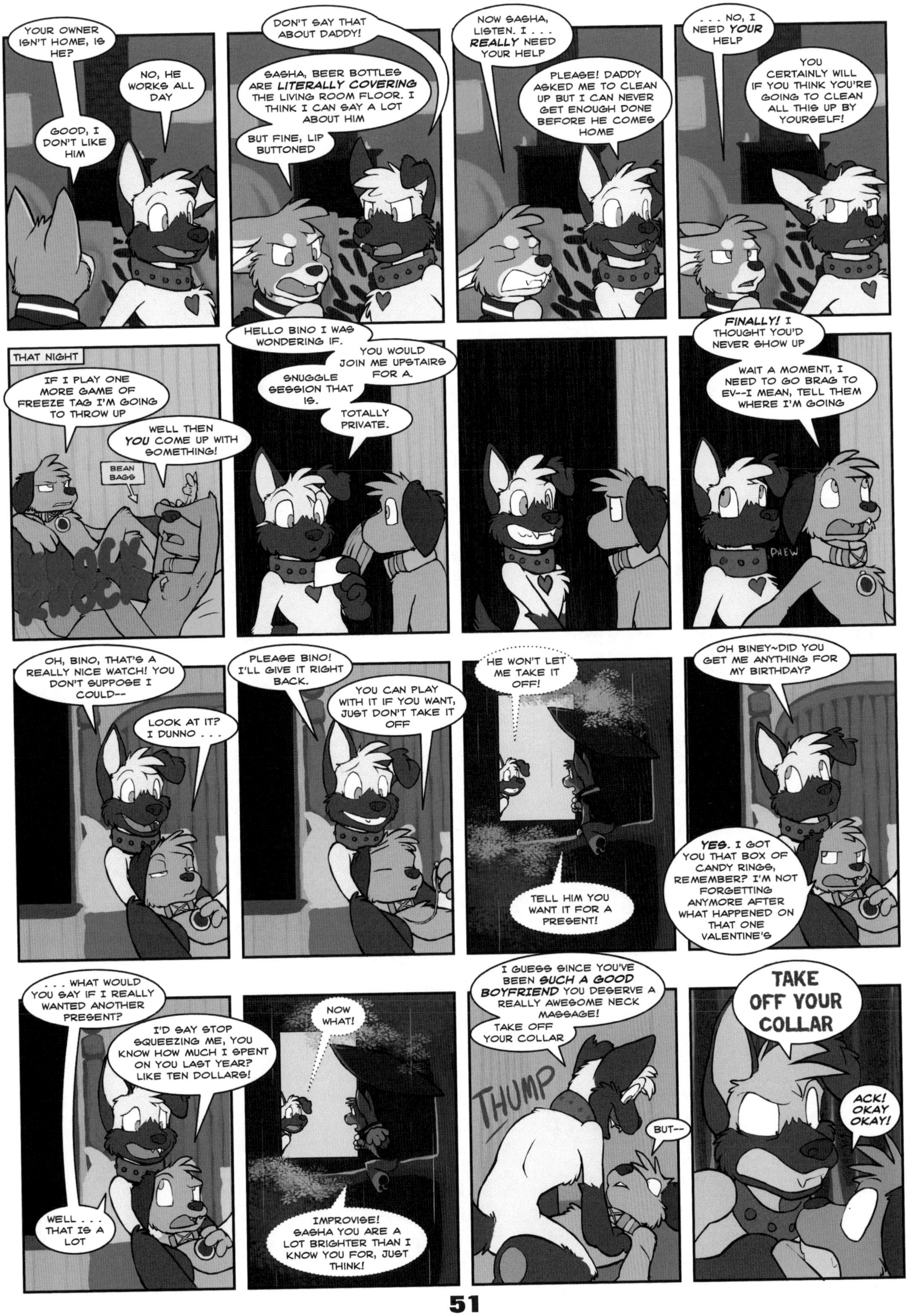
YOUR OWNER ISN'T HOME, IS HE?
NO, HE WORKS ALL DAY
GOOD, I DON'T LIKE HIM
DON'T SAY THAT ABOUT DADDY!
SASHA, BEER BOTTLES ARE LITERALLY COVERING THE LIVING ROOM FLOOR. I THINK I CAN SAY A LOT ABOUT HIM
BUT FINE, LIP BUTTONED
NOW SASHA, LISTEN. I . . . REALLY NEED YOUR HELP
PLEASE! DADDY ASKED ME TO CLEAN UP BUT I CAN NEVER GET ENOUGH DONE BEFORE HE COMES HOME
. . . NO, I NEED YOUR HELP
YOU CERTAINLY WILL IF YOU THINK YOU'RE GOING TO CLEAN ALL THIS UP BY YOURSELF!
THAT NIGHT
IF I PLAY ONE MORE GAME OF FREEZE TAG I'M GOING TO THROW UP
WELL THEN YOU COME UP WITH SOMETHING!
BEAN BAGS
KNOCK KNOCK
HELLO BINO I WAS WONDERING IF.
YOU WOULD JOIN ME UPSTAIRS FOR A.
SNUGGLE SESSION THAT IS.
TOTALLY PRIVATE.
FINALLY! I THOUGHT YOU'D NEVER SHOW UP
WAIT A MOMENT, I NEED TO GO BRAG TO EV--I MEAN, TELL THEM WHERE I'M GOING
PHEW
OH, BINO, THAT'S A REALLY NICE WATCH! YOU DON'T SUPPOSE I COULD--
LOOK AT IT? I DUNNO . . .
PLEASE BINO! I'LL GIVE IT RIGHT BACK.
YOU CAN PLAY WITH IT IF YOU WANT, JUST DON'T TAKE IT OFF
HE WON'T LET ME TAKE IT OFF!
TELL HIM YOU WANT IT FOR A PRESENT!
OH BINEY~DID YOU GET ME ANYTHING FOR MY BIRTHDAY?
YES. I GOT YOU THAT BOX OF CANDY RINGS, REMEMBER? I'M NOT FORGETTING ANYMORE AFTER WHAT HAPPENED ON THAT ONE VALENTINE'S
. . . WHAT WOULD YOU SAY IF I REALLY WANTED ANOTHER PRESENT?
I'D SAY STOP SQUEEZING ME, YOU KNOW HOW MUCH I SPENT ON YOU LAST YEAR? LIKE TEN DOLLARS!
WELL . . . THAT IS A LOT
NOW WHAT!
IMPROVISE! SASHA YOU ARE A LOT BRIGHTER THAN I KNOW YOU FOR, JUST THINK!
I GUESS SINCE YOU'VE BEEN SUCH A GOOD BOYFRIEND YOU DESERVE A REALLY AWESOME NECK MASSAGE!
TAKE OFF YOUR COLLAR
THUMP
BUT--
TAKE OFF YOUR COLLAR
ACK! OKAY OKAY!

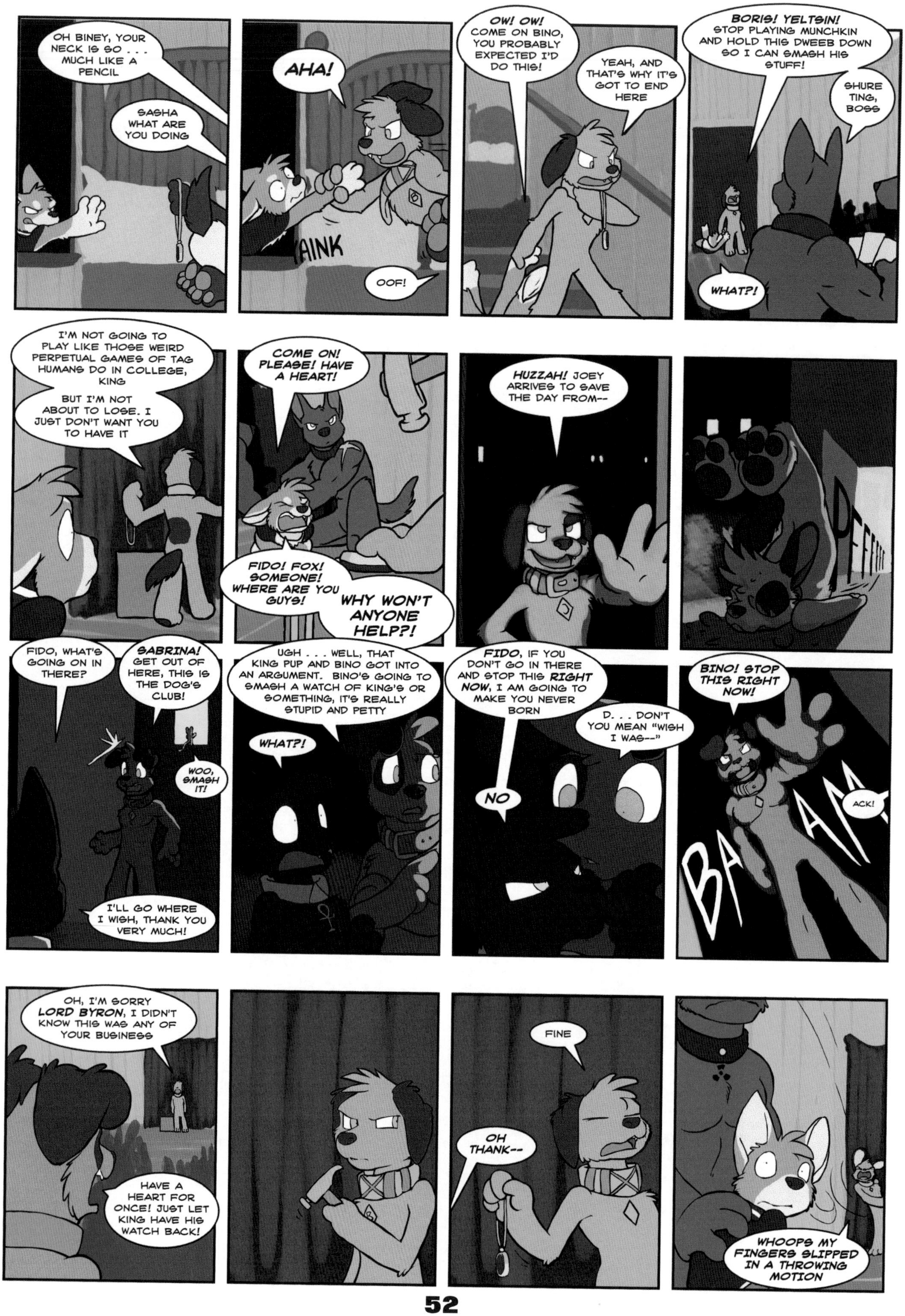

OH BINEY, YOUR NECK IS SO . . . MUCH LIKE A PENCIL
SASHA WHAT ARE YOU DOING
AHA!
YAINK
OOF!
OW! OW! COME ON BINO, YOU PROBABLY EXPECTED I'D DO THIS!
YEAH, AND THAT'S WHY IT'S GOT TO END HERE
BORIS! YELTSIN! STOP PLAYING MUNCHKIN AND HOLD THIS DWEEB DOWN SO I CAN SMASH HIS STUFF!
SHURE TING, BOSS
WHAT?!
I'M NOT GOING TO PLAY LIKE THOSE WEIRD PERPETUAL GAMES OF TAG HUMANS DO IN COLLEGE, KING
BUT I'M NOT ABOUT TO LOSE. I JUST DON'T WANT YOU TO HAVE IT
COME ON! PLEASE! HAVE A HEART!
FIDO! FOX! SOMEONE! WHERE ARE YOU GUYS!
WHY WON'T ANYONE HELP?!
HUZZAH! JOEY ARRIVES TO SAVE THE DAY FROM--
PFFFFFT
FIDO, WHAT'S GOING ON IN THERE?
SABRINA! GET OUT OF HERE, THIS IS THE DOG'S CLUB!
WOO, SMASH IT!
I'LL GO WHERE I WISH, THANK YOU VERY MUCH!
UGH . . . WELL, THAT KING PUP AND BINO GOT INTO AN ARGUMENT. BINO'S GOING TO SMASH A WATCH OF KING'S OR SOMETHING, IT'S REALLY STUPID AND PETTY
WHAT?!
FIDO, IF YOU DON'T GO IN THERE AND STOP THIS RIGHT NOW, I AM GOING TO MAKE YOU NEVER BORN
D. . . DON'T YOU MEAN "WISH I WAS--"
NO
BINO! STOP THIS RIGHT NOW!
BAAM!
ACK!
OH, I'M SORRY LORD BYRON, I DIDN'T KNOW THIS WAS ANY OF YOUR BUSINESS
HAVE A HEART FOR ONCE! JUST LET KING HAVE HIS WATCH BACK!
FINE
OH THANK--
WHOOPS MY FINGERS SLIPPED IN A THROWING MOTION

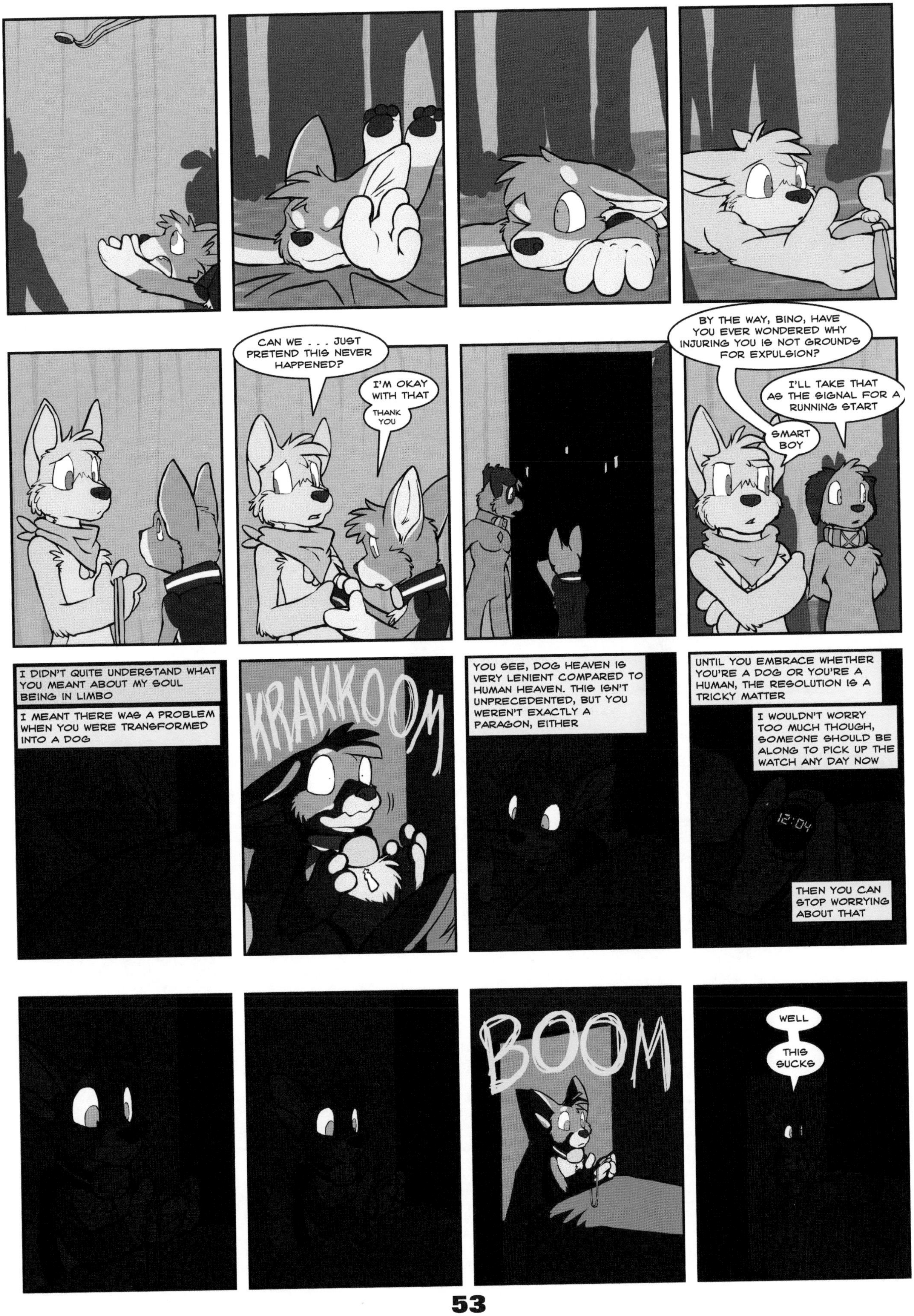
CAN WE . . . JUST PRETEND THIS NEVER HAPPENED?
I'M OKAY WITH THAT
THANK YOU
BY THE WAY, BINO, HAVE YOU EVER WONDERED WHY INJURING YOU IS NOT GROUNDS FOR EXPULSION?
SMART BOY
I'LL TAKE THAT AS THE SIGNAL FOR A RUNNING START
I DIDN'T QUITE UNDERSTAND WHAT YOU MEANT ABOUT MY SOUL BEING IN LIMBO
I MEANT THERE WAS A PROBLEM WHEN YOU WERE TRANSFORMED INTO A DOG
KRAKKOOM
YOU SEE, DOG HEAVEN IS VERY LENIENT COMPARED TO HUMAN HEAVEN. THIS ISN'T UNPRECEDENTED, BUT YOU WEREN'T EXACTLY A PARAGON, EITHER
UNTIL YOU EMBRACE WHETHER YOU'RE A DOG OR YOU'RE A HUMAN, THE RESOLUTION IS A TRICKY MATTER
I WOULDN'T WORRY TOO MUCH THOUGH, SOMEONE SHOULD BE ALONG TO PICK UP THE WATCH ANY DAY NOW
12:04
THEN YOU CAN STOP WORRYING ABOUT THAT
BOOM
WELL
THIS SUCKS

KING and his collection of EMBARRASSING OUTFITS

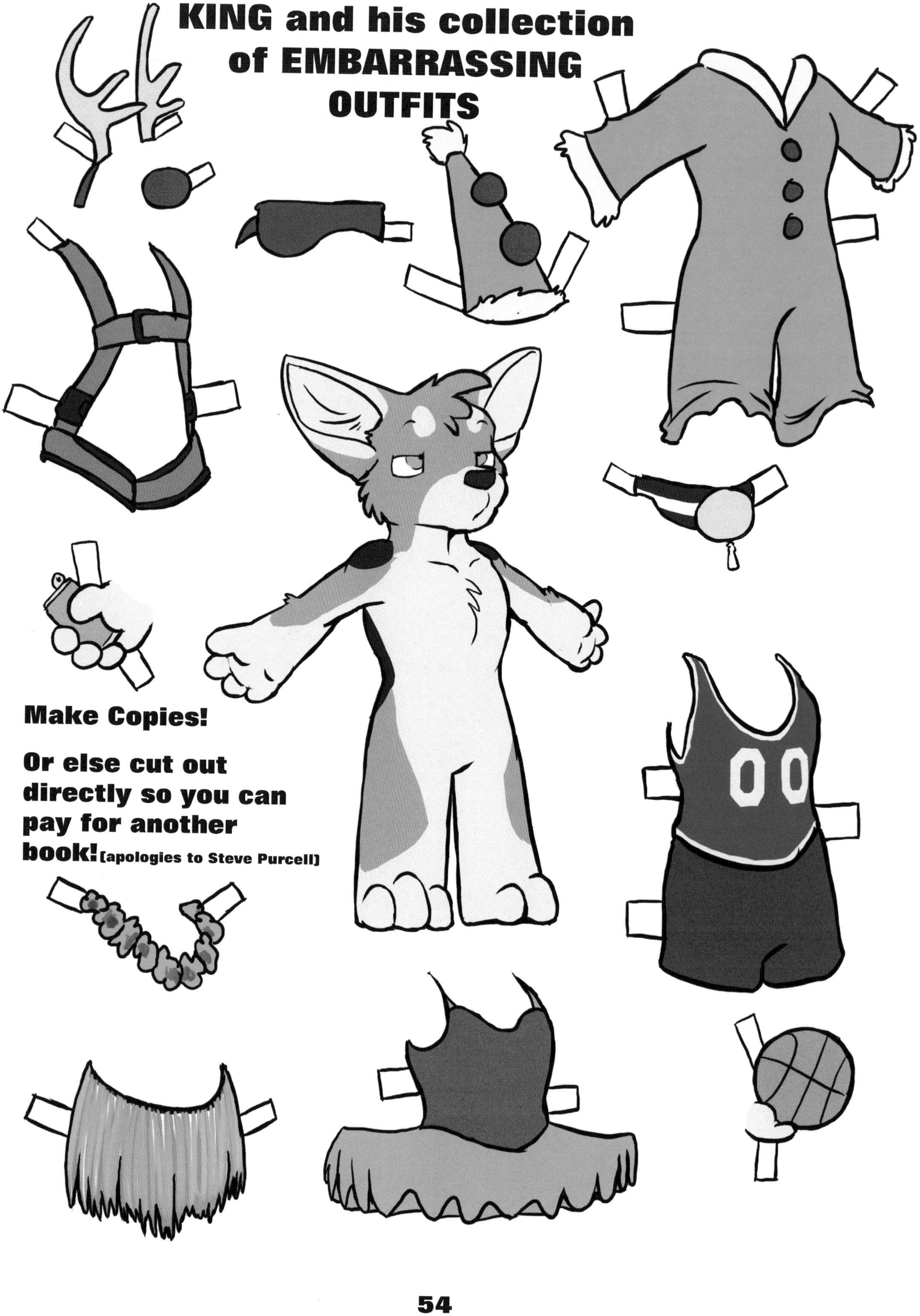
00

Make Copies!

Or else cut out directly so you can pay for another book! [apologies to Steve Purcell]

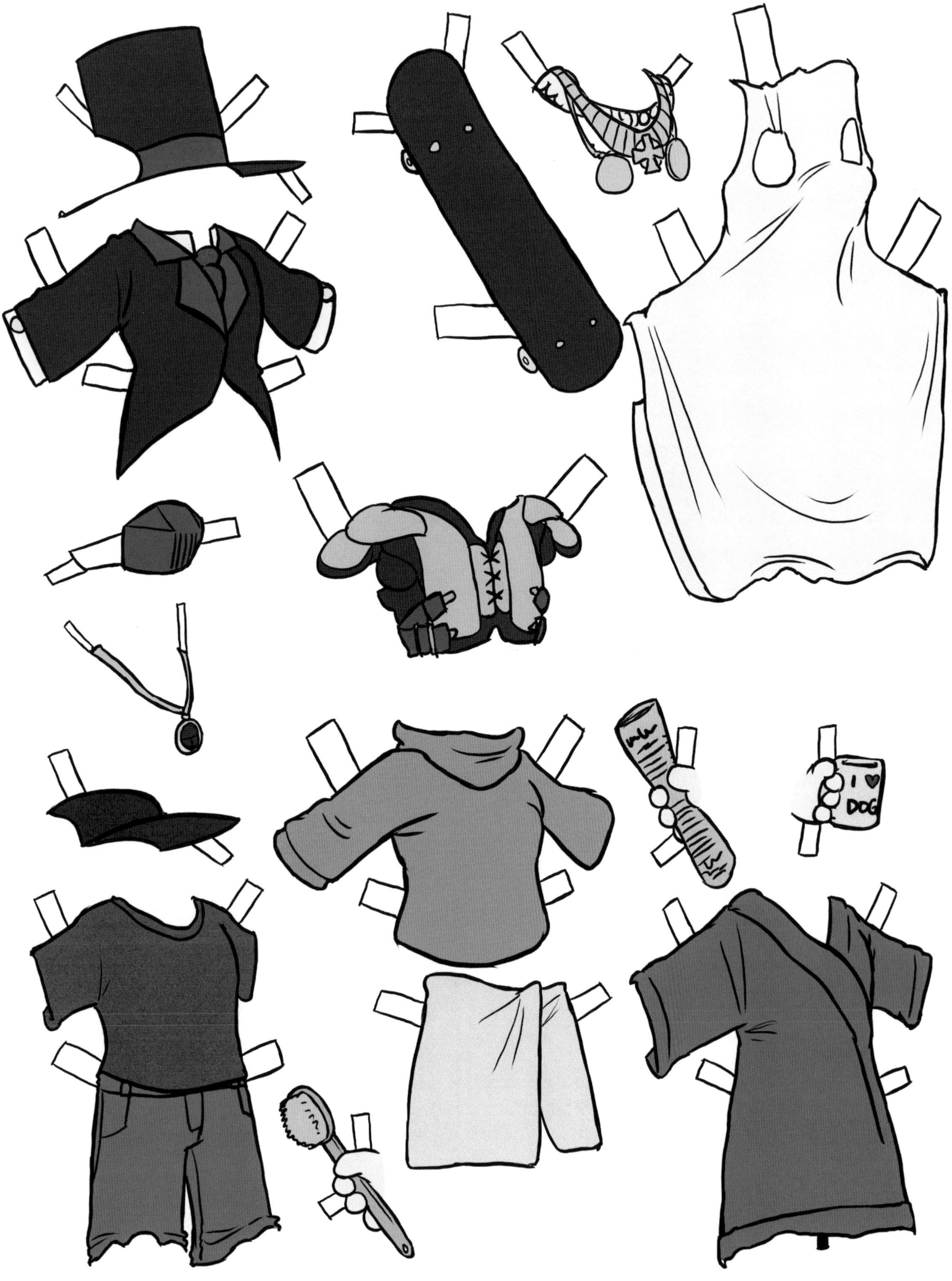
I ♥ DOG

Next time, on

Housepets!

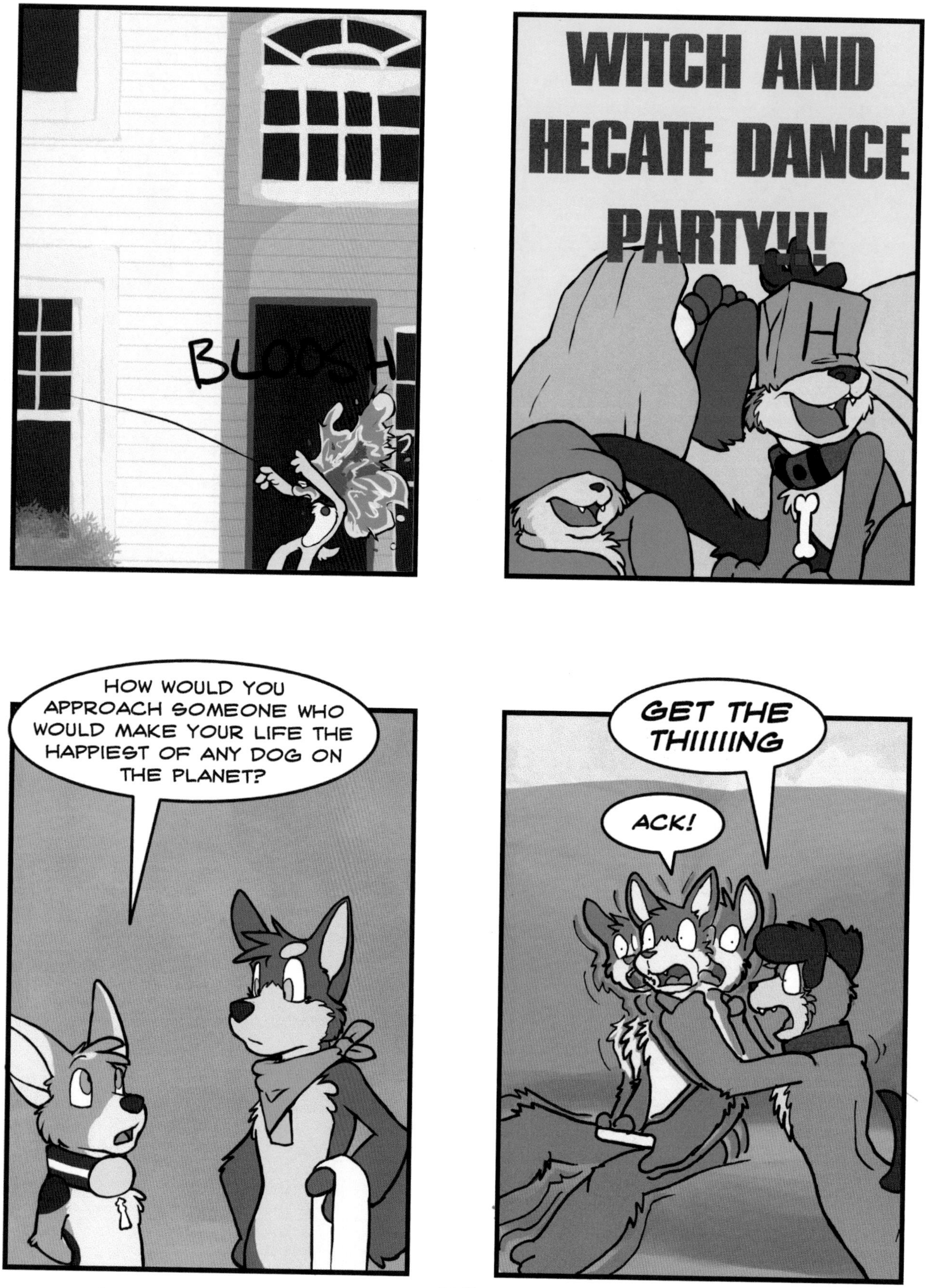

BLOOSH
WITCH AND HECATE DANCE PARTY!!!
HOW WOULD YOU APPROACH SOMEONE WHO WOULD MAKE YOUR LIFE THE HAPPIEST OF ANY DOG ON THE PLANET?
GET THE THIIIIING
ACK!

Made in the USA
Lexington, KY
27 December 2013